1972

This book may be kept

FOURTEEN DAYS

A fine will be charged for each day the book is kept overtime.

GAYLORD 142			PRINTED IN U.S.A.

AMERICA'S LOST PLAYS

XXI
SATIRIC COMEDIES

The original twenty-volume series of America's Lost Plays was published by Princeton University Press in 1940 and reissued in ten volumes, 1963–65, by Indiana University Press. *Satiric Comedies* is a new addition to this series.

Satiric Comedies

EDITED BY

WALTER J. MESERVE
and
WILLIAM R. REARDON

INDIANA UNIVERSITY PRESS
BLOOMINGTON   LONDON

CONTENTS

INTRODUCTION

FOLKLORE SUPPORTS THE IDEA that from very early times the human spirit has reacted in some fashion against overdoses of solemnity. In the history of theatre the earliest such manifestations were perhaps the satirical improvisations on phallic themes which became in time both the old comedy and the satyr dramas. Later variations include the Feast of Fools, the racy ditties of minstrels, jongleurs, and troubadours, and numerous mocking parodies.

In America satirists maintained the tradition in the writing of blue verses, biting parodies, and the songs and skits of minstrels. And, with equal concern for tradition, there were those who objected, like William Bradford in 1630:

> And Morton became Lord of Misrule, and maintained (as it were) a schoole of Athisme. . . . They also set up a May-pole, drinking and dancing aboute it . . . as if they had anew revived and celebrated the feasts of the Roman Goddess Flora. . . . Morton likewise (to shew his poetric) composed sundry rimes and verses, some tending to lasciviousness, and others to the detraction and scandall of some persons, which he affixed to this idle or idoll May-polle.[1]

Morton was sent back to England on the next boat, but even book burnings (1654),[2] monopoly on the printing press (1662, 1664),[3] condemnations of rogues and vagabonds, prohibitions against games and plays (1699),[4] or establishment of Watch and Ward societies (1699)[5] failed to suppress the ribaldry. Finally, in 1712, "An Act Against Intemperance, Immorality, and Profaneness, and For Reformation of Manners" appeared.[6] The prototype for all censorship laws in the United States, this act was obviously the result of rather flagrant activity. One section in particular indicates the seriousness of the law makers as well as the scope and success of the satirists.

> And whereas evil communication, wicked, profane, impure, filthy and obscene songs, composures, writings or prints, do corrupt the mind, and are incentives to all manner of impieties and debaucheries, more especially when digested, composed or uttered in imitation or mockery of devotion or religious exercises . . . whosoever shall be convicted of writing, printing, publishing of any filthy, obscene, or profane song, pamphlet, libel or mock sermon, in imitation or in mimicking of preaching, or any other part of divine worship . . . shall be punished by fine . . . not exceeding twenty pounds, or by standing on the pillory once or

oftener, with an inscription of his crime in capital letters affixed over his head . . .[7]

Satirists very early recognized the theatre as a congenial place for their efforts. Although they may have at first used satire to veil their opinions, dramatists eventually admitted their purposes. In *Daranzel; or, The Persian Patriot* (1800) David Everett noted that "a playhouse is an ample field for satire" but urged that it be used "without ill nature." That other dramatists did not agree completely with Everett is obvious in this collection. The gamut was run—from the grim to the ribald to gentle ridicule. The objects of attack included almost every aspect of government and society. Bawdy satire was most common during and before the Revolution, but it remained a persistent part of American drama. Benign satire, probably because it could show the theatre as a corrective and moral influence upon society, soon became a major part of theatrical fare. Playwrights such as Mrs. Suzanna Rowson stated their objectives clearly: "It has been my endeavor to place social virtues in the fairest point of view, and hold up, to merited contempt and ridicule, their [the people's] vices."[8] Throughout the nineteenth century in America (and, of course, on to the present day) satire has been one of the most acceptable of theatrical techniques.

One has the impression that the early American playwrights, theatre hacks as they obviously were, had great pleasure in their work. Artistry was perhaps the last thing that concerned them, and yet they possessed knowledge of their craft and certainly an understanding of theatre audiences. The theatre is always a mirror of society, but the immediacy of that reflection in eighteenth and nineteenth century American drama is startling. Let an action in Congress, a border war, or a social event occur—anything that stirred the public—and the chances for a play on the subject within a short time were reasonably good. And the play was an opportunity for commentary, satirical or otherwise.

Political and governmental activities have often been fertile ground for the satirists. Mercy Warren's bitter satires on the Revolution—*The Adulateur* (1773), *The Group* (1775)—well illustrate the capacity for caustic criticism of a cultured and witty lady. Cruder in thought and language is *The Blockheads; or, The Affrighted Officers* (1776), by an anonymous playwright. Samuel Low's *The Politician Outwitted* (1788) is a satirical farce, while John Murdock's *The Politician; or, The State of Things* (1798) satirizes the bitter factional spirit during Washington's second administration. *The Triumphs of Love; or, Happy Reconciliation* (1795), another Murdock play, uses satire to comment on a number of socio-political problems, particularly taxes. *Federalism Triumphant in the Steady Habits of Connecticut Alone; or, The Turnpike Road to Fortune* (1802), by Leonard Chester, satirizes politics in Connecticut, and J. H. Nichols' *Jefferson and Liberty* (1801) ridicules John Adams as the Duke of Braintree. With the creation of Major Jack Downing by Seba Smith in the early 1820's, politicians and political issues continued a life of burlesque which did not end with "Wintergreen for President" in Kaufman and Ryskind's *Of Thee I Sing* (1931).

All aspects of social life provided the dramatist with materials for either titillating or torturing his audiences. The stage Yankee was, of course, a ridiculed character, but not painfully so. The American who affected English ways and the foreigner were treated much more severely from *The Contrast* (1787) through Samuel Woodworth's *The Forest Rose* (1825) to *Fashion* (1845), as was America's too-ready acceptance of foreign fashion in *The Better Sort* (1879), anonymous. In several plays, written at a time when war was unpopular, the soldier was crudely lashed. A character in Robert Munford's *The Patriots* (1789) says that "gaming and whoring are the first qualifications of a soldier." Religion was also attacked (Joseph Croswell's *A New World Planted,* 1802) and professional men were satirized (John Beete's *The Man of the Times,* 1797). Lawyers were particularly open to calumny, being classed with drunkards and brothel-keepers in an early Connecticut law. Education was assaulted in such plays as A. B. Lindsley's *Love and Friendship* (1809) and Samuel Randall's *The Sophomore* (1812). During the years when the theatre was much closer to the people than it is today, few attitudes of society escaped the man who was trying to make a little money in the theatre, and his first reaction seemed to be to ridicule what he saw.

Governor Robert Hunter's *Androboros* (1714) has the distinction of being the first play printed in the United States. The facts behind its creation—concerning the factionalism of colonial politics in New York—are clearly described by Lawrence Leder.[9] Hunter had been extremely angered and frustrated by certain individuals, and writing the play was his way of getting some satisfaction. Even without specific knowledge of the contemporary circumstances, however, the play is enjoyable. Considering themselves beyond the law of the land, the Assembly is a collection of incredibly self-centered imbeciles who delight in ridiculous proposals and in utter confusion. Equally obnoxious is the venal clergy. Though the adherents of common sense triumph in the play, it was a savage personal revenge for Hunter, who gave no indication that the establishment was capable of change or betterment.

Although historians of American drama and theatre have given the play only slight attention, it is certainly one of America's robust satires. No record exists of a performance of *Androboros,* and the play is usually considered a closet drama. It might, however, have been performed by Hunter and his friends, staged perhaps in a large living room under very simple conditions. Unquestionably, some people would happily have accommodated Hunter. In fact, in 1714, the very year *Androboros* was printed, Samuel Sewall was stunned at the suggestion that a play be performed in the Council Chamber in staid Boston.

The farcical effects utilized are theatrically successful. Euchred into believing that he is dead, Androboros is insulted, mocked, knocked down, belched upon, hit with foul water, poked with brooms, sprinkled with dust, sprayed with beer, blinded with snuff, and dumped into a collapsing chair. In addition to these outright farcical effects, the standard weapons of the satirist, from invective through wit, are liberally present throughout. Hunter's manipulated characters also reiterate his satirical point, because the clergy, represented by Fizle, sinks down into the trap with Androboros. Certainly there is enough theatricality in this play to make one cautious about assuming that it was not presented.

The text of *Androboros* (meaning man-eater) included in this collection is from the only known extant copy, preserved in the Huntington Library. The hand-inked changes, thought to be made by Hunter, are incorporated, along with the identification of the play characters, also presumably made by Hunter.

Not much can be said about *The Trial of Atticus Before Justice Beau for a Rape* (1771). It managed to be preserved, but the facts of its creation did not. Nor do we know anything about its stage history, if indeed it was ever performed. The major theatrical virtue of this satire is the happy idea upon which the play focuses: the ludicrous rape. There is also some skill in characterization, which is fairly effective in delineating the hypocrisies. As with most trial plays, this one could easily have been staged, as the action is limited primarily to the court room. The author, however, displays a minimal theatrical awareness; there is a lack of theatrical inventiveness as he utilizes only the standard devices. Even while satirizing the religious fanatic, he protests that he means "no reflection on religion or any of the sincere professors of it, of what denomination whatever." But the play achieves its main goal: a forceful depiction of the pettiness of the local colonial court. A group of stubborn New Englanders of the calibre of Giles Corey of Salem would surely have enjoyed acting or watching this satirical farce.

The attack, in *The Trial of Atticus,* is on the venality of the courts and lawyers who support the slander and hypocrisy in the community. Atticus, something of the modern anti-hero, is moderately dissolute and exceptionally stubborn. Certainly he does not frighten easily. Against him are arrayed a particularly debased group: a judge and a lawyer more interested in fees than in due process, and unsavory witnesses with only petty and unrelated grievances. With a corrupt institution and a slanderous community as the background, the author tells his ridiculous story of a two-year-old rape that never occurred. Once again, as in Androboros, the establishment is shown in a hopeless condition, and the author gives no hope for clearing the courts of venality or altering the slanderous attitude of the people.

Like *The Trial of Atticus, The Battle of Brooklyn* (1776) is by an unknown author, and although there is no substantial evidence that it was performed, one might, in spite of its blatant propaganda and weak theatrical effect, assume with a certain confidence that it was. Other strongly partisan Loyalist plays saw the stage, and there are records which testify that British soldiers under Generals Howe and Burgoyne thoroughly enjoyed attending the theatre. General Burgoyne even contributed to the satirical attacks on the Continental forces with *The Blockade of Boston* (1775). Since the Revolution was not a popular war with the Boston and New York mercantile class, plays against it were readily printed. *The Americans Roused in a Cure for the Spleen* (1775), which is simply a Tory tract in dialogue, is attributed to Jonathan Sewall, a well-known Tory. The title page of *The Battle of Brooklyn* indicates that it was printed for J. Rivington, a notorious New York Tory. Although the ridicule in this play is more ribald than in other extant plays, *The Battle of Brooklyn* certainly indicates that there must have been other plays of a similar nature by people with the influence and the interest to see their work performed.

The main emphasis of *The Battle of Brooklyn* is on the cowardly attitudes and the drunken propensities of the American officers, which the author sneers at rather than ridicules. Such dialogue lacks humor, while throughout the play there is little indication of wit. In addition, the play is not very theatrical. Only occasionally is there a dramatic moment, such as Remsen's appearance after fleeing the battle. There is some attempt at dramatized humor, however, as when Stirling is brought on stage half-dressed, but for the most part the script is light on action and heavy on description of action. Likewise, the satire lacks finesse. The political structure of the American rebels is presented as founded on lechers, drunkards, horse thieves, counterfeiters, and cowards, while religion is referred to in a degrading manner.

Without question the play is a scurrilous representation of the American Revolution, the rebel generals, and the grasping Continental Congress out to acquire power and riches at the expense of the natives. Since the leaders from Washington on down are delineated as totally unsavory characters, the entire establishment of the Revolution is viewed as destructive for the people.

Darby's Return (1789) was written by William Dunlap (1766–1839), who is generally referred to as the Father of American Drama. Undoubtedly he deserves this distinction. He was the first professional dramatist in America, having some fifty-three plays to his credit (thirty-nine either wholly or partially original, the remainder adaptations and translations). Although, like numerous others, he eventually went bankrupt as a theatre manager, his years with the John Street and Park Theatres in New York (1796–1804) showed him to be a conscientious man who learned as he worked in the theatre. His most significant contribution to both American drama and theatre is *A History of the American Theatre* (1832), a narrative of his observations which, though sometimes in error, are invaluable to American scholars. Although he was not the great dramatist that some of his contemporaries considered him, he was a serious and able pioneer who brought respectability to the American theatre.

Certainly he did not consider *Darby's Return* one of his serious efforts, as were *The Father* (1788), *André* (1798), or *Leicester* (1806). In fact, he prefaced his publication of the play with a note "To the Public":

The following Dramatic trifle was not written for publication, but merely to serve the Gentleman [the actor Thomas Wignell] on whose night it was performed. The Author is fully sensible, that the plea of its being a hasty Production is no excuse for obtruding on the Public an incorrect Composition; but, being importuned by his Friends, he has consented to throw this Child of the Day on the protection of the World, encouraged by the flattering reception it received at the Theatre, and the candour once before shewn to its Author.

Certain lines were omitted in the acted version but restored for the printed text.

In his *History*,[10] Dunlap recounted how Wignell, in preparing for his benefit performance, asked for a play using the character of Darby from John O'Keeffe's *The Poor Soldier*. The result was "an interlude, in which Darby, after various adventures in Europe and in the United States, returns to Ireland and recounts the sights he had seen. This trifle was called *Darby's Return*, and was for years extremely popular, and several times published." It was first produced on November 24, 1789, with the following cast:

DARBY	MR. WIGNELL
DERMOT	MR. WOOLLS
CLOWN	MR. RYAN
FATHER LUKE	MR. BIDDLE
OLD WOMAN	MRS. HAMILTON
KATHLEEN	MRS. MORRIS

The play was well received; in fact, on December 15, 1789, Lewis Hallam chose it for his benefit, which is a rather good indication of the play's success. *The Gazette of the United States* for November 28, 1789, noted that *Darby's Return* was replete with happy allusions to interesting events and "very delicately turned compliments. On the appearance of THE PRESIDENT, the audience rose and received him with the warmest acclamations—the genuine effusions of the hearts of FREEMEN." The reaction of the President to one scene in the play was evidently a glittering moment in Dunlap's life. In telling of his experiences in America, Darby was asked to describe the President, at which point Washington, sitting in the audience, looked a bit serious (according to Dunlap), and braced himself for the usual eulogy; but Darby missed seeing "the great man," who, from his theatre box, indulged in "a hearty laugh."

In contrast to other satires of this period, *Darby's Return* is a very gentle satire of the "galant" soldier who has returned to his little village. In the mode of a century which disliked the idea of military service and considered those who followed it to be wastrels, Dunlap indicates that the romantic conception of the soldier is not based on any actual military activities. The technique is narrative rather than dramatic, and the skit does not show Dunlap's later craftsmanship, but with song and dance it boasts a fairly theatrical opening and closing. It is, in every sense of the word, a trifle, and within that framework makes its point about the military.

John Brougham's burlesque of the Pocahontas story was one of the best of this very popular genre in mid-nineteenth century America. Many a successful play was subjected to this ridiculous mocking or parody. Bulwer-Lytton's *The Lady of Lyons,* for example, was anonymously burlesqued as *The Lady of Irons* (1842); Dion Boucicault's *London Assurance* was travestied by "Phaz" as *New Orleans Assurance* (1842) and by Silas Steele as *Philadelphia Assurance* (1841); Boucicault's *Octoroon* also appeared in a Southern version called *The Moctoroon.* On February 21, 1857, the *Spirit of the Times* announced a new burlesque of *Medea* entitled *My-Deary* to be produced at Purdy's National Theatre in New York. Augustin Daly's very popular *Under the Gaslight* was burlesqued as *Under the Cairo-seen Lamp Post*

(1867). Not only plays were parodied; sometimes a poem supplied the source of material, such as that burlesqued by Charles M. Walcot's *Hiawatha; or, Ardent Spirits and Laughing Water* (1856), or a play might be based on the deeds or personality of a famous figure, such as Columbus.

In any kind of burlesque or parody John Brougham (1810–1880) was a master, and Laurence Hutton dubbed him the "Aristophanes" of the American stage.[11] From his first appearance in America in 1842, after some success in London, until his death, he was one of the best of the actor-manager-playwrights of this period. Joe Jefferson was impressed with him as a comic actor, particularly in Irish character roles. As a writer of burlesques and Irish plays Brougham also showed considerable wit and talent in the seventy-five or more plays recorded to him. As a manager his experiences carried him through a variety of theatres—Brougham's Lyceum and Brougham's Bowery being memorable, along with his efforts in the opera house built by Jim Fisk and Daniel Drew, who eventually felt the bite of his ire and Irish wit. In the area of farce-comedy and parody he is the one outstanding writer in nineteenth century America.

Brougham is generally remembered because he almost single-handedly brought an end to the tremendously popular plays which celebrated the heroic American Indian with his *Metamora; or, The Last of the Pollywogs* (1847) and *Po-Ca-Hon-Tas; or, The Gentle Savage* (1855). His talent for burlesque, however, was broader in scope and, according to some critics, more effective in other plays. It was with *Metamora,* however, that Brougham found new success and added burlesque to his usual performance of the Irish character in his own Irish plays. He was quick to see his advantage, as his tremendous productivity suggests. On March 15, 1851, the *Spirit of the Times* reviewed the hit at Brougham's Lyceum: "the new romantic, neoromantic, gyromantic, operatic, hippodramatic, and heterogeneous burlesque spectacle, founded on the recent *transparent* circumstances, and called 'Ye Deville and Dr. Faustus.'" The *Spirit* critic considered "broad burlesque his *forte*" and found the play filled with "capital satires upon recent doings of the city authorities." Another of his very successful burlesques was *Columbus El Filibustero,* produced at Burton's New Theatre in New York on January 9, 1858, which the *Spirit of the Times* critic said abounded in puns, witticisms, poetic language, "in fact, a little of everything between the extremes of sublime and ridiculous." Brougham's performance as Columbus was considered far superior to his acting in *Pocahontas.* Acorn, the *Spirit* critic in Boston, was never given to unwarranted enthusiasm, but when *Columbus* came to Boston (June, 1858), he saw Brougham as "not only an artist of some versatility, but a man of true genius."

On December 24, 1855, *Po-Ca-Hon-Tas* opened at Wallack's Theatre in

New York: "a most uproarious burlesque," according to the critic of the New York *Daily Times* (December 24, 1855, p. 4), who had read the play, "written by that most uproarious of actors, Mr. John Brougham . . . with decided and deserved success." Odell called it "the biggest success of the winter, here or anywhere."[12] Hornblow said it was "one of the most successful burlesques of its kind ever seen on the American stage."[13] When it was produced at Niblo's in January, 1856, it was described as "a palpable hit." Brougham made the most of it throughout his career, while others also produced it in many American cities. Whether or not it is Brougham's best burlesque, the piece is excellent comic satire and places Brougham firmly in that great tradition.

Po-Ca-Hon-Tas is a burlesque of a literary fetish—the Indian play. Although no particular institution is singled out for attack, Brougham provides a broadside of satire on a variety of topics, including New York politics, the current theatre, and social posturing. As might be expected, it contains many theatrical devices: song and dance, incipient fights, pistol shots, dangerously pointed arrows, humorous costumes, and word play. The King sings in the finale, "Take our bad jokes in good humor." Brougham set out to reduce the Pocahontas legend to an absurdity and succeeded admirably.

Writers of satiric comedies may have the personal satisfaction of exercising great freedom while working within a substantial artistic tradition. Dunlap and Brougham are representative of hundreds of lesser writers within the same genre. Their work, although not significant as literature, is quantitatively important in the history of eighteenth and nineteenth century American theatre. From the robust ridicule of the law in *The Trial of Atticus*, of the clergy and politicians in *Androboros*, and of the Revolution in *The Battle of Brooklyn*, to the gentle ribbing of the soldier's life in *Darby's Return* and the broader satire on the theatre and numerous aspects of social life in *Po-Ca-Hon-Tas*, these plays show clearly the development of one kind of American drama. They illustrate the principal objectives of the satirist during this period and in their chronology suggest the greater particularity and sophistication that separate the work of Brougham from that of the author of *The Trial of Atticus*. No writer in the nineteenth century wrote more satiric comedies with greater success than Brougham, and he set a style which led to such writers as George Ade and George S. Kaufman. The five plays reprinted in this volume establish the beginnings of a genre in American drama.

WALTER J. MESERVE
WILLIAM R. REARDON

NOTES

1. William Bradford, *History of Plymouth Plantation, 1620–1647* (Boston. Published for the Mass. Historical Society by Houghton Mifflin, 1912), II, 46.

2. *Ancient Charter, Colony, and Province Laws of Mass. Bay* (Boston. Thomas Wait for the Commonwealth, 1814). Cf. Colony Laws: Chapter LI, Section 3, 121.

3. Ibid., Appendix. Chapter IV, Section I and II, "Acts Restraining the Press."

4. Ibid., Cf. Province Laws. Chapter LXIII, 334–338.

5. Ibid., Chapter LXV.

6. Ibid., Chapter CV, 395–399.

7. Ibid. Cf. Sections 7 and 8 of law.

8. S. H. Rowson, "Preface," *Slaves in Algiers; or, A Struggle for Freedom,* Philadelphia, 1794.

9. Lawrence H. Leder, "Robert Hunter's *Androboros*," *Bulletin of the New York Public Library,* LXVIII (March, 1964), 153–160.

10. William Dunlap, *A History of the American Theatre* (New York. J. & J. Harper, 1832), I, 160–161.

11. Laurence Hutton, *Curiosities of the American Stage* (New York: Harper & Brothers, 1891), 164.

12. George C. D. Odell, *Annals of the New York Stage* (New York: Columbia University Press, 1927–49), VI, 433.

13. Arthur Hornblow, *A History of the Theatre in America* (Philadelphia: J. B. Lippincott Co., 1919), II, 188.

AMERICA'S LOST PLAYS

XXI
SATIRIC COMEDIES

ANDROBOROS

A Biographical Farce in Three Acts, VIZ.

The SENATE,

The CONSISTORY,

and

The APOTHEOSIS

By Governour Hunter

Printed at Moropolis since 1st August, 1714

DRAMMATIS PERSONÆ

ANDROBOROS. [GENERAL FRANCIS NICHOLSON, 1655–1728]

KEEPER. [GOVERNOR ROBERT HUNTER, d. 1734]

DEPUTY. [GEORGE CLARK, 1676–1760]

SPEAKER. [WILLIAM NICOLLS, 1655–1723]

ÆSOP. [DAVID JAMISON, 1660–1739]

DOODLESACK. [ABRAHAM LAKERMAN]

TOM OF BEDLAM.

BABILARD. [SAMUEL BAYARD]

COXCOMB. [DANIEL COXE, 1673–1739]

MULLIGRUB. [SAMUEL MULFORD, 1645–1725]

COBUS. [JACOBUS VAN CORTLANDT, 1658–1739]

SOLEMN. [LEWIS MORRIS, 1671–1746]

DOOR-KEEPER.

FIZLE. [REV. WILLIAM VESEY, 1674–1746]

FLIP. [ADOLPH PHILIPSE, 1665–1750]

MESSENGER.

SCENE: Long Gallary in Moor-Fields.

THE DEDICATION
TO
DON. COM. FIZ.

Right Dreadful SIR!

CErdo Gloucestriensis, an Author of the last Century, of great Sagacity, observ'd well, That Runto Polimunto Plumpismenoi Raperpandico —— What d'ye stare at? This is good Greek for ought you know, and contains a Mystery, which shall continue so, unless you Reveal it; and so no more of that. The following Elionophysalo Fizlical Farce having fallen into my Hands by a most surprizing Accident, it seemeth meet unto me that it should, with all due Reverence Kiss yours. Here it lies at your Feet, take it up. Now read the first Act, —— Have ye done? What's the matter Man? Have ye got the Gripes? A Plague on your Sower Faces. Bring him a Dram. What have you to do, had you to do, or ought you to have to do with the *Senate?* You smell a Rat, you say. Be it so. But compose your self, and now Read the second Act, —— How d'ye like it, ha? O Hooo, T'churrrrrrrrrtch, I can say that as Loud as you can do; and if you'll but leave out these Damnable R's and T's which make it so hard in Pronounciation, and harder in Digestion, I like it better than you do. You don't believe me! and I don't believe in you; and this is a perilous Article in a Mans Belief too; For one who dy'd a very good Christian, was sentenc'd by your Sanctity to be bury'd a Pagan, only because he seem'd to believe that you were some-what Thick of believing; yet you are a Christian, a very good Christian,

> *So was your Leader, Major Weere*
> *Burnt for Bu—ry, God be here.*

He had a good Gift of the Gob too: You were bred up in the same Accademy, the same Principles, and the same way of Worship: All the Difference between you lies in this nice point, He Worship't the Dev'l instead of God, and you worship God as if he were the Dev'l. Come to't again, first take two Turns cross the Room, Cross-ways, I say, Wipe the Sweat from your Brows, and sit down. Now read the Third Act, I'll sing the while,

It is an Old Maxim, et c'est Escrit,
Au trou de mon cul, look there you'll sie't,
When the Head is 'Be—ck't the Body's Beshit,
Which no Body dare Deny, Deny,
Which no Body dare Deny.

Read on, and be hang'd, don't mind me, Man, I sing for my own Diversion.

But 'tis strange how Notions are chang'd of late,
For 'tis a New Maxim, but an odd one, That
Ce que pend a nos culs doit nous garnir latete,
That I flatly and boldly Deny, Deny,
That I flatly and boldly Deny.

What is the Matter now? Is he Dead? or is't a Qualm? Holo, a Hay! Who waits there? some burn't Feathers, *Sal Armoniack?* No, No, Let him smell to the Skirt of his own Garment. So, he Recovers. Poor Fiz! who could have thought that you were so quick of Smelling! Come, Man, take Courage; What have You or I to do with it? Let the Gall'd Horse wince, our Withers are unwrung. But tell me, will you be quiet for the Future? You shall be paid for't, nay, you have been paid for't; and it is hard that Men must be Brib'd for Not doing what they ought Not to do. I remember an Odd Fellow upon *Pont Neuf* who got his Livelihood by as Odd a Stratagem; He procur'd himself a Portable Forge and Bellows, which he carried under his Cloak, and having heated a small Iron red hot, he would lug it out and present it to the Gentlemen who pass'd that way, with his Complement, *Good Sir! Pray Sir! give me leave to run my hot Iron into your Arse.* When the Gentlemen started at the Extravagance and Danger of the Motion, he continued, *Nay, Sir, if you don't like it, pay me but a Sol Marquee for the heating of my Iron, and there is no harm done.* Now had he insisted upon the Performance of the Operation aforesaid, after payment for the necessary Apparatus, he deserv'd to have his Bones broke; but he was most commonly satisfied, and all the Consequence was a fit of Laughter. Now, I know that it is not an easie matter for you to get rid of your Forge and Bellows, but can't you blow your Bellows and heat your Iron at home, and quit that unaccountable Rage of Runing it into your honest quiet Neighbours Arses, who pay you amply, and meerly for Forbearance? But I have done. Peace be with ye, I mean such a one as he made who made you a COM-

And it was a most Masterly stroke of Art
  To give Fizle Room to Act his part;
For a Fizle restrain'd will bounce like a F——t,
    Which no Body can Deny, Deny,
    Which no Body can Deny.
But when it Escapes from Canonical Hose
  And fly's in your Face, as it's odds it does,
That a Man should be hang'd for stopping his Nose,
    That I flatly and boldly Deny, Deny;
    That I flatly and boldly Deny.
Long kept under Hatches, 'twill force a Vent
  In the Shape of a Turd, with its Size and Scent
And perhaps in its way may beshit a Vestment,[1]
    Which no body can Deny, Deny;
    Which no body can Deny.
But However 'tis Dignify'd or Disguis'd,
  That it should be for that the higher Priz'd,
And either Don Commis'd or Canoniz'd,
    That I flatly and boldly Deny, Deny,
    That I flatly and boldly Deny.

B'UEY FIZLE.

ACT I.

SCENE I: *Keeper, Deputy and Tom.*

DEPUTY. I Hope, Sir, it is not your intention that this same Senate, as they call it, should sit.

KEEPER. What harm is there in't, if it does?

DEPUTY. No great harm, only 'twill feed[2] their Frenzy; They are big with Expectation of some mighty Deliverance, towards which is to be brought about by means of *Androboros;* I think they call him so; Whether there is or ever was such a Person, I know not: but all their hopes are placed in him.

TOM. Sir, it is *Old Nick-nack,* who has Paganiz'd himself with that Name, which interpreted, signifies a *Man-Eater.* He is now very far gone indeed, He talks of nothing but Battles and Seiges, tho' he never saw one, and Conquests over Nations, and Alliances with Princes who never had a being; and this Senate is mainly intended for his Reception. I hope you will not forbid its Meeting, if you do, I shall loose an Employment, having had the Honor to be appointed Clerk of the Senate this Morning, after the Choice of the Speaker; so I beg you'll not Rob me of that Honor, and your self of some Diversion, and I shall take care that their Session shall be harmless.

KEEPER. I wish you Joy with all my heart; But Prethee, *Tom,* What Chance or evil Fate conducted thee to this same Doleful Mansion? I am surpriz'd to find thee in such Company.

TOM. No Chance, I assure you, *Sir,* but free Choice. I found in my reading, That Man was composed of three parts, *Body, Soul* and *Spirit,* and that the two first were entirely ingross'd by two Societys, so I Resolv'd to Exercise my poor Talent upon the Infirmitys of the last, not with any hopes or intention to Cure them, but as others do, meerly to raise my self a Maintenance out of them, here under your Honors happy Auspeces. But, Lo, here they come. Retire to a Corner. If I am seen in your Company, my Project is spoyl'd.

SCENE II: *Enter Doodlesack, Babilard, Solemn, Æsop, &c.*

SPEAKER. Gentlemen, The Honor you have done me, how little soever I may deserve it, lays me under an Obligation to Exert my self to the utmost for the interest of this House. I humbly propose, That in the first place we concert and agree upon some necessary Rules for preventing Confusion.

DEPUTY. [*Aside*] Well spoke, Mr. Speaker. Tho' 'tis something strange that he who has ever affirm'd, That Laws and Liberty were things Incompatible, should now propose to proceed by Rules.

MULLIGR. I desire to be heard before you proceed to Rules, or any thing else; I have a Speech ready.

DOODLESACK. Laet onse hearken to Mr. Speaker, and begin with some Rules.

MULLIG. I'll have my Speech first.

COXCOMB. D——n your Speech, Let's proceed to Rules.

BABILARD. If Rules be necessary to the Speech, let us have the Speech first, but if the Speech be necessary to the Rules, let us have the Rules.

COX. I'm for neither Speech nor Rules, let us fall upon buss'ness.

SPEAKER. Gentlemen, The Question is not, as I take it, which you'll be pleas'd to have, but which shall have the Preference; for you may have both in their Turns.

ALL. [*Confusedly*] Speech, Rules; Rules, Speech, &c.

MULLIGRUB. My Speech has carry'd it. Hum, Ha, Ough, Ough, Ough, Ough, &c.

COX. Rot ye, it was not your Cough that Carry'd it; Let off your Speech.

ÆSOP. Mr. Speaker, I do not find that this matter is, as yet, determin'd to the full satisfaction of this House, for which Cause I beg leave to offer an Expedient, which will end the Debate, that is, That we may have both at a time; whilst Mr. *Mulligrub* is Exonerating himself, we may imploy ourselves in adjusting and forming the necessary Rules.

ALL. Agreed.

SPEAKER. Mr. *Mulligrub,* You may proceed.

MULL. Gentlemen, The ill Measures that have been taken, and the Foundation that hath been laid within this Tenement, to make the Tenants thereof, Tenants therein, is the Cause which causeth me to make this Speech. Our Grievances being innumerable, I shall Enumerate them. The first I shall mention, is this, That tho' the Tenement be large, the Mansions many, and the Inhabitants Numerous, There is but One Kitchin, and one Cellar, by which means we are kept from Eating and drinking What we please, When we please, and as Much as we please, which is our Birth-Right Priviledge by the Laws of God and Nature, settled upon us by Act of Parliment; for which cause I humbly [illegible half line] House Whether it may not be more Convenient that each Mansion have its proper Kitchin and Cellar under the special Direction of the respective Tenants?

To clear up the Necessity of this Method, I'll tell you what happ'ned to me t'other day; One of the Servants of this House, who brought me a Mess of Water Gruel, being my special Friend, and knowing how eagerly my Stomach stood towards what was forbidden me by the Physitians, conveys a Hand of Pork into the Porrige, but being discover'd he was punisht, tho' he offer'd to take his Corporal Oath, That the Hand of Pork was a bunch of Radishes. But of all others, we of the East End of the Tenement suffer most, for by reason of our distance from the Kitchin, our Porrige is cold before it comes to our Hands. To Remedy this, we fell upon a private Intercourse with the Bethlemites on the other side of Moor-fields, who by virtue of their Charter run at large, by which we broke the Laws pretty Comfortably for a season; but these same subtle Fellows of the Kitchin found it out, and put a stop to't, to the Great Prejudice of the Freedom of the Subject, and the direct Discouragement of our indirect Commerce. I Remember we once Address'd our Superiors, That we might have a Servant of our own, independent of this Plaguey Keeper; They were Graciously pleas'd to allow us such a one, with this Restriction only, That the Servant aforesaid might have the Custody of our Straw and Water, but by no means of our Meat and Drink; notwithstanding this, the Keeper will not permit him to take the care and Custody of our Victuals and Drink. What! does he think us *Non Corpus Mentlus,* that we do not know the meaning of plain words! But I shall Conclude at this time, with this Exhortation, That since it appears plainly, that we of this Tenement, who are the Tenants thereof, are in danger of Being, by the Foundations laid, made Tenants therein, let us not lie Crying thereat, but be Valiant Therefore, and Vindicate our Rights There-from, Our Birth-Right Parliamentary Rights, settled upon us by the Ten Commandments.

SPEAKER. Gentlemen, Mr. Mulligrub has given you time to Concert the Rules of the House, would you have them read by the Clerk, in the Order they have been given to him by the several Members?

ALL. Ay, Ay.

TOM. [*Reads*] Mr. *Speaker* Proposes, That to prevent Confusion, not above Three or Four at most be permitted to speak at Once, except in a Grand Committee, where there is no occasion of Hearers.

Mr. *Coxcomb* humbly proposes, That no Body be allow'd to speak but himself, because for want of the Attentive Faculty, he is like to have no share in the Hearing, and so ought to have Compensation in Speaking.

Doodlesack has given his in a Forreign Tongue, which when interpreted stands thus, That He having but a small share of Elocution, but a very lively and strong imagination, may have leave, as occasion shall Offer, to Express his Thoughts by Staring, Grinning and Grimacing, of which he has so

Exquisite a Talent, that those who cannot be said to understand any thing else, perfectly understand him in that Method of Utterance.

Babilardus Represents, That he is quite Dum-founded by the late fall of Stocks, so in Order to the opening his Mouth, he proposes a Law for raising Int'rest to *Twelve per Cent.*

Æsop has given his Rule in Rhime, as follows,
>   The Rule that I would advise,
>   Is, Be quiet, and eat your Bread,
>   If 'tis good; To be Merry and Wise.
>   'Tis the Dev'l to be Sullen and Mad.

Coxcomb.   Damn all Rules, Let us proceed to buss'ness.

Cobus.   Laet onze erst come to some Revoluties.

Coxcom.   Resolutions! Ay, begin with that, I like that Motion well enough; it is the shortest way.

Speaker.   Let one at a time Propose, and the rest Agree or Dissent, as they think fit.

Coxcom.   Resolv'd That neither this House, or they whom we Represent are bound by any Laws, Rules or Customs, any Law, Rule or Custom to the Contrary Notwithstanding.

All.   Agreed.

Mulligr.   That this House disclaims all Powers, Preheminencies or Authoritys, except it's own.

All.   Agreed.

Babilard.   That this House has an Inherent and Undoubted Right to the Undoubted Property of those we Represent.

Coxcomb.   That this House is the only Undoubted Supreme Inferior and Infimus Court of this Tenement, and that all others are a Nusance.

All.   Agreed.

Solemn.   Mr. Speaker, being Resolv'd to enter my Dissent to these several Resolves, I shall first give my Reasons for so doing. I believe it is needless to put you in mind of our Origine, from whence we sprang, and how we came hither. It is well known that we were of that Number of Publick Spirited Persons, distinguish't from our Neighbours by an inward Light or Faculty, call it what you Please. The *Romans* call it *Æstrum,* the *French, Verve,* our Northern Nation has indeed given it a Courser Name, which gave us a strong Disposition toward Reformations, Remonstrations, Resolutions, and other Acts of Zeal; in the eager pursuit of which we were apt to throw our selves, sometimes our Neighbours, into the Fire or Water. The Wisdom of the Times thought fit to Erect this tenement for our Intertainment, where the Exercize of the Faculty aforesaid might be less Dangerous or hurtful to our selves, or others. Here we are Maintain'd at their Charge with Food and Rayment suitable to our Condition, and the Fabrick kept in Repair at the no small Annual Expences of our Land-Lords. And what Returns do we make? Have not many of us from our private Cells thrown our Filth and Ordure in their Faces? And now in a Collective Body we are about to throw more filthy Resolves at them.

ALL. To the Barr, to the Barr.

ALL. No, With-draw, With-draw.

SOLEMN. I desire to be heard.

ALL. With-draw.

SPEAKER. *Sir,* It is the pleasure of this House that you With-draw, in order to your being heard. [*Exit Solemn*] Gentlemen, your have heard this mans Insolence. What shall be done with him?

COXCOMB. Hang'd, Drawn and Quarter'd.

ÆSOP. Ay, but what is his Crime?

COXCOM. For affronting the Majesty of this House.

ÆSOP. In what? What has he done or said?

COBUS. Dat weet ick niet, but I agree with *Coxcombs* Propositie.

SPEAKER. I am for Inflicting no Punishment but what is in our power, that is, to Expell him the House.

ALL. Expell, Expell.

ÆSOP. Hold a little, I suppose you intend to punish him, and not your selves; I'll tell you a Story.

ALL. Expell, Expell, &c.

ÆSOP. I beg your patience, 'tis but a short one; it is a Tale of a Pack of Hounds of my Acquantance,

> *Fowler,* the stanchest Hound o'th' breed,
>   Had got th' ill Will of all the rest;
> Not for his Tongue, his Nose or Speed,
>   Tho' these were all by far the best;
>   Malice and Envy know no bounds
>   And Currs have ever bark'd at Hounds.
> But that which most provok'd their Spite
>   Was this, that when they run a Foil
> Or Counter, *Fowler* led them right,
>   Which cost him many a bitter broil,

Snubbing the Rash and Rioters,
And lugging laizy Ones by th' Ears.

So at a General Council held
    For Grievances, or what you will,
Poor trusty *Fowler* was Expell'd,
    That free-born Dogs might range their fill.
        And so they did; but mark what came on't,
        Hence-forth they made but sorry Game on't.
The giddy Pack, their Guide b'ing gone,
    Run Riot, and the Hunts-Man swore,
Strap't some, and some he whipt; but one
    He hang'd, a Noisy babling Curr.
        In short, the Pack was spoyl'd; Pray then,
        Shall *Fowler* be Expell'd agen?

COXCOMB. A Pox on your Tale, let us proceed to the Vote.

SPEAKER. What is then your pleasure with relation to the Member who is to be Expell'd?

ALL. Expell'd, Expell'd.

SPEAKER. Call him to the Bar. [*Enter Solemn*] Sir, For *Reasons* best known to our selves, you are Expell'd.

SOLEMN. *Sir,* You do me too much honor. [*Exit. Enter Messenger*]

MESSENGER. Mr. *Speaker,* The Lord *Androboros* with Two Men in Black desires Admittance.

SPEAKER. Is it your pleasure he be admitted?

OMNES. Ay, Ay.

SPEAKER. Let the Clerk go to him with the Compliments of the House, and Conduct him in. [*Tom a going*]

KEEPER. St. St. St. *Tom,* a Word with you. Pray who are these same men in Black, who accompany the General?

TOM. Two other special Friends of yours, *viz. Fizle* and *Flip;* The first was heretofore a *Muggletonian* of the other side of *Moore-fields,* but having no Butter to his Bread there, he Chang'd their *Service* for that of this House; He sometime fancy'd himself to be the Pope, but his Brother not relishing that as Derogatory to his Pretentions, he is now Contended to be Patriarch of the Western Empire, of which *Androboros* is to be Sultan; The other, for a wonderful Energy in the two most Unruly Members of the Body, has been follow'd of late by the Women and Boys, but a late sinistrous Accident has

Crack't his Voice, and—that now he is but little regarded. But I must be gone. [*Ex. Tom*]

KEEPER. The Rogue is a good Painter.

DEPUTY. He draws from the Life, I assure you.

SCENE III: *Enter Androboros and Tom, Flip and Fizle.*

ANDROB. Most Venerable Gentlemen, Upon my Rounds of Inspection, Prospection and Retrospection, I have understood with Pleasure, that you have sequester'd from your House that wandering Plague, that Kibes in the Heels, and Piles in the posteriors of Mankind.

ÆSOP. Pardon me, Sir, your Name has not been mention'd here, that I know of.

ANDROB. I mean *Solemn,* which Act I approve and Commend. It is with no less satisfaction that I now acquaint you, That upon the Earnest Application and most humble Suit of the High and Potent *Towrowmow-youghtough,* Emperor of many Nations, and my good Allies, the Kings of *Agnisagkimaghswoughsayk, Savanaghtipheugh,* and *Bowwougewouffe,* I have undertaken an Expedition against the *Mulo Machians,* your Inveterate Foes. Your Concurrence to enable me to carry it on with Success, is what I demand and expect; and for your Incouragement, I do swear by this sacred Image, not to pare these Nails, wash this blew Visage, or put off the speckled *Shirt,* Until I have made that Haughly Monarch Confess himself, in all his Projects for Universal Dominion, my Inferior, and My Delamya, fairer then the fairest Princess of his Blood or Empire. So leaving this weighty Affair to your wise Counsels, We bid you heartily Farewell. [*Exit Strutting*]

SPEAKER. You have heard what this Man has propos'd. What do you Resolve?

COXCOM. Let us Resolve to Support, Maintain and Defend the undoubted Title of the Great *Androboros* to the Powers and Authoritys he has Graciously Assum'd over this and all other the like Tenements, against all Wardens, Directors, Keepers, and their Abettors.

ALL. Agreed.

DOODLESACK. Laet onze Dissolve, That a Summ not Exceeding Negen Skillingen and Elleve Pence be rais'd for the Expeditie.

ALL. Agreed.

SPEAKER. Ay, and 'tis more than 'tis worth.

BABILARD. Let us Resolve, That He has behav'd Himself on the said Expedition with Courage, Conduct and Prudence.

SPEAKER. What! before 'tis over!

ÆSOP. By all means, lest when it is over you should have less reason for this Resolve. But if after all, we must go to War, I would be glad to be better satisfy'd with the Choice of a Leader; For as to this Mans Prowess, we have nothing but his own Word for't.

COXCOMB. The Choice is a good Choice, and he that doubts it, is a Son — So for that, amongst other weighty Reasons, I second Mr. *Babilards* Motion.

DOODLESACK. Ick ock, because it may cast some Reflectie upon our Keeper.

ÆSOP. Before you proceed any further, I'll beg leave to tell you another Tale, it is but a short one, and if it fails to Instruct, it may divert.

> The *Bees* so fam'd for Feats of War,
>   And Arts of Peace, were once, of Sense
> As void as other Insects are,
>   'Till time and late Experience,
>   The only Schoolmaster of Fools,
>   Taught them the use of Laws and Rules.

> In that wild state they were Assail'd
>   By th' Wasps, oft routed and Opprest;
> Not that their Hearts or Hands had fail'd,
>   But that their Head was none o'th' best,
>   The *Drone* being, by the Commons Voice,
>   Chose for the Greatness of his Noise.

> Thus ill they sped in every Battle;
>   For tho' the Chief was in Request
> At home, for's Fools Coat and his Rattle,
>   Abroad he was the Common Jest.
>   The *Wasps* in all Ingagements, held—
>   His Folly more then half the Field.

> Grown Wiser by repeated Woes,
>   The Bees thought fit to change their Chief,
> It was a *Humble Bee* they Chose,
>   Whose Conduct brought them quick Relief;
>   And ever since that Race has led 'em,
>   The *Drones* are Drums, as Nature made 'em.

But go on with your Resolves; you have mine.

SPEAKER. I like the last Choice of the Bees, for my part; for by the Law no man can be allow'd to be an Evidence for himself, especially when he happens to be a single one.

DOODLESACK. Wishy Washy's; I agree to Mr. *Babilards* Propositie, for the Reasons given, with this addition, That our Keeper is een Skellum.

COXCOMB. And ought to be dismiss't from having any further Autho[rity] over us.

SCENE IV: *Enter Keeper and Deputy.*

KEEPER. To your Kennels, ye Hounds.—[*Exit Omnes*]

DEPUTY. Now, *Sir,* I hope you are satisfied, and for the future you'll keep 'em to their Cells.

KEEPER. No, let them enjoy their former Liberty, perhaps they'll stand Corrected.

DEPUTY. I much doubt it; but I shall Obey.

KEEPER. Now, Mr. *Tom.* If I may be so bold, Favour me with a sight of the Minutes of your House.

TOM. With all my heart, here they are.

KEEPER. What's here! A *Castle,* a *Wind-Mill,* and *Shephard* with a *Ram* at his back?

TOM. Ay, *Sir,* a sort of Ægyptian short Hand, containing the substance of their Resolves. The *Castle Renvers'd* and in the Air, denotes the independency of our House; The *Wind-Mill* without Sails, an Expedition without Means or Leader; and the *Ram* butting the *Shephard on the Breech,* or in other words, dismissing him from having any further Authority over him.—

KEEPER. That wants no Explanation. You'll Watch them, *Tom,* and serve them in the same Capacity, if they meet again.

TOM. To the best of my Skill.

KEEPER. Let's to Dinner.   [*Exeunt*]

ACT II.

SCENE I: *Enter Babilard, Fizle, Flip, Coxcomb.*

BABILARD. You see what our wise Resolves have brought upon us, we shall never do his buss'ness in this way, Muzled as we are; I wish my Advice had been follow'd.

FIZLE. Pray what was that?

BABILARD. I was for proceeding in the way of secret Representations and Remonstrances against him, which My Lord Oinobaros,[3] his declar'd Enemy, might have long e'er this improv'd to his Ruin.

FIZLE. That was my own Method, but that which discourages me is, that at Parting my Lord assur'd me, That he would return in six Moneths, and Confirm me in my Patriarchat; instead of that, he has himself taken up with the Wardenship of a Spunging-house.

COXCOMB. No, that Method will never do. Have not I, and my Friends transmitted to Mr. *Wry Rump*[4] a Ream of Complaints, as big as the Bunch on his back, which were Referr'd to the Consideration of the Casually sitting Members of the little House, and he was dismiss'd with a Kick o'th' Breech. We must Accuse him of something more Flagrant; Triffles won't do.

FIZLE. Why, Then I have another Device for you. You see he can Dissolve our Senate with a Crack of his Whip, so there is nothing to be done that way. Let us incorporate our selves into a *Consistory;* That I believe He dare not touch, without being Reputed an Enemy to the Consistory; and if he does, we may hunt him down full Cry at present.

FLIP. That I shold like well enough, but I'm afraid the Cunning Rogue won't meddle with us, as such.

FIZLE. We'll say, and swear, That he did, and that's all one. I have a Plot in my head, which I hope will do the buss'ness; in the mean time, go you and aquaint the Rest, that they meet us here in full Consistory Immediately. [*Exit Babilard, and Coxcom*]

FLIP. Pray, Brother, Instruct me in your Contrivance, I may help you out with my Advice.

FIZLE. It is briefly this. This same Rogue was ever an Enemy to the short Coats and Scanty Skirts of the Laity, and Consequently to the long Robes and Pudding Sleeves of the others; I'll instantly have my long Coat Beskirted and Besh——, and give out, That it is He, or some of his People, who has don't. If any should be so Heterodox as to doubt the truth o'nt, I have some ready to swear to the Size and Color of the T——.

FLIP. I like this well; about it streight, I'll attend them here, Open the Consistory in your Name, and Prepare 'em for what is to ensue. [*Exit Fizle*]

FLIP. This same Fizle is a Notable Fellow for the head of a Consistory, if he had but a Competent Doze of Brains; but These are so shallow that a Louse may suck 'em up without surfeiting, which renders that noble Portion of *Malice*, with which he is Liberally endow'd of little use to the Publick.

SCENE II: *Enter Mulligrub, Doodlesack, Babilard, Coxcomb, Tom, Æsop, &c.*

FLIP. In the Absence of My Brother *Fizle* whose occasions have call'd him away for a little time, I am to acquaint you, That he has of his own free Will, meer Motion and by virtue of the Plenitude of his Patriarchal Authority, chosen and elected you for his Consistory-men and Counsellors in all Cases and Causes Visable and Invisable.

COXCOM. We are highly honor'd by his Choice, and Promise an Implicit Obedience to his pleasure. [*Enter Fizle*]

FIZLE. O Horror! O Abomination! was ever the like seen, heard or read of!

FLIP. What's the Matter?

FIZLE. As I went to Robe my self for the more decent Attendance on this Consistory I found my Robes in this Pickle! That Vestment, so Reverenc'd by the Antient and Modern World, beskirted and Bedaub'd with what I must not name!

ÆSOP. Who has done this?

FIZLE. Who has done it! Who but the known Enemies to Consistorys and Long Skirts?

ÆSOP. But methinks your Discretion should have directed you to our Keeper with this Complaint.

FIZLE. Our Keeper! One of my Brethren told him of it but now, and he coldly Reply'd, If Mr. *Fizle* from the Redundancy of his Zeal has beshit himself, the Abundance of his Wisdom, methinks, should prevail with him to keep the Secret, and make himself Clean.

MULLIGR. A plain Proof the Keeper is the Man.

COXCOMB. Ay, Ay, There Needs No Other Proof; it must be the Keeper.

FIZLE. I own, I thought so from the beginning; but what course shall we steer for Redress?

FLIP. If I may be thought worthy to advise in a matter of this Moment, we shall immediately Address My Lord Oinobaros on this head, he being a Devotee to Long Robes of both Gendres, must highly Resent this Affront, and with the Assistance of *Androboros,* no less an Enemy to the Keeper, may Manage it to his Ruin and our Satisfaction.

BABIL. Let *Mr. Fizle* draw up an Address, and we'll all sign it.

FIZLE. Gentlemen, If such is your pleasure, I'll retire with the Clerk, prepare one, and submit it to your Approbation.

ALL. Pray go about it. [*Exit Fizle and Tom*]

ÆSOP. I Resent this Affront to the Long Robe as much as any Man, but methinks you proceed too hastily, and upon too slender Grounds against your Keeper. We all know the Malice of Mr. *Fizle's* heart, and that it has Increas'd in proportion to the Keepers good Nature. Had he been oftner Check'd, he had been less Troublesome to himself and us. Let us not provoke our Keeper; for my part, I think he is a good one.

COXCOM. What! is he not an Enemy to the Consistory?

ÆSOP. No, he is an Enemy to their Folly, and can well distinguish between the Function and the Person who abuses it. Pray give me leave to divert you, 'till *Fizle* returns, with another Tale; It is harmless, and I hope will give no Offence.

> In the beginning God made Men,
>   And all was well, but in the End
> Men made their Gods, and Fondly pay'd 'em.
>   The Worship due to him that made 'em,
> And all was wrong; for they Increas'd,
>   And Multiply'd like Man and Beast.
> But none were bold in Reverence
>   So much as *Phoebus,* God of sense
> And Non-sense, Patron, as occasion
>   Did serve, of Arts and Inspiration.
> Once on a day as he was led
>   About to give a Cast of's Trade,
> Whether to Dance, or Sing, or Fiddle,
>   Or as some say, to read a Riddle,
> I know not; but what-e'er it was,
>   His Vehicle was but an Ass,
> And he none of the wisest neither;
>   For when the Crowd had got together

To pay due Homage to their God,
    Strowing with Flow'rs the Path he rode,
And singing Paans, the vain Beast
    Believ'd all this, to him Address't:
He Pranc'd, and Flung, and Frisk'd about,
    Scatt'ring much Dirt among the Rout,
And bray'd as if h' had got a Pack
    Of Dev'ls, and not a God on's back.
The Crowd essay'd by gentle ways,
    To Curb his Pride, and smooth his Pace;
But all was talking to the Wind;
    For Zeal is deaf, when-e'er 'tis blind.
Finding all other Methods fails,
    They seiz'd him by the Ears and Tail,
And took the Idol from his back,
    With many a lusty Bang and Thwack.
They let him know, that *Phoebus* was
    The God, and he was but an Ass.

How d'ye like it? It is an old Tale, but a true *Eccum Ipsum;* let him speak for himself.

Scene III: *Enter Fizle and Tom.*

Fizle. Gentlemen, I have finish'd the Address. Is it your pleasure that the Clerk read it?

All. Ay, Ay.

Tom. [*Reads*] To the most Potent Lord *Oinobaros,* Count of *Kynomma-tia,* Baron of *Elaphokardia,* The General Consistory of *New Bed-l-m* most Humbly Represent, That we your Excellencies ever *Besorted Subjects,*

Fizle. Devoted Subjects.

Tom. Under a deep sense of the manifold *Bastings* we Enjoy'd.

Fizle. *Blessings,* you Ouph you.

Tom. Blessings we Enjoy'd under your *Wild Administration.*

Fizle. Mild Administration.

Tom. Mild Administration, find our selves at this time under a *Nonsensical Inclination.*

Fizle. What's that? Let me see't, *Non-sensical Inclination!* It can't be so; It is *Indispensible Obligation.*

Tom. Ay, it should be so.

Fizle. Write it down so then.

Tom. 'Tis done. Finding our selves under an *Incomprehensible Obstination.*

Flip. 'Owns! That's worse than t'other.

Tom. Cry Mercy, That is a blunder, *Indispensible Obligation* to have Recourse to your Excellencies known *Condemnable Opposition* to our Consistory, and all Things Sacred.

Fizle. I think the Dev'l is in the Fellow. It is *Commendable Disposition.*

Tom. You use so many Long Words, that a Clerk who is not a Scholar may easily mistake one for another. Towards our Consistory, and all things Sacred, Take leave humble to Represent, That on the *Ev'ning which succeeded the following Day.*

Fizle. Thou Eternal Dunce! *The Ev'ning which preceded All-hallowday.*

Tom. Which preceded *All-hallowday* some open or secret Enemies to this Consistory broke into our *Cupboard.*

Fizle. Ward-Robe.

Tom. Wardrobe, taking from thence some Lumber appertaining to the *Chief of our Rogues,* I mean, some Robes appertaining to the Chief of our Number, which they Inhumanely Tore to pieces and Bedaub'd with *Odour.*

Mulligrub. Hold! I make Exception to that, for there are sweet Odors as well as sower.

Flip. 'Slid; 'tis *Ordure,* (and not *Odour*) which is but another Name for a T——d.

Mulligr. Write it down so then, for a T—— is a T—— all the world over.

Æsop. And the more you stir it, the more 'twill stink. But go on.

Tom. Now tho' we *cannot Possibly Prove,* yet we *Affirm Positively,* That it is our Keeper.

Æsop. How's that?

Fizle. He reads wrong; it is, *Tho' we cannot Positively Prove,* yet *we Affirm,* That *possibly it may be our Keeper.* Go on.

Tom. Our Keeper, or some of his People, who is guilty of this *Facetious Fact.*

Fizle. Flagitious Fact.

Tom. Flagitious Fact. We further beg leave to Represent, That this Morning in a Collective Body, by a great *Brutality of Noises.*

Fizle. Plurality of Voices.

Tom. We had declar'd him a *Raskal,* but he had the Impudence to send us packing to our Cells, though we had several *Merduous Matters* under the *Infection of our Hose*.

MULLIGRUB.   Hold! I do not well understand that, Read it again.

FIZLE.   He cant read his own Hand; it is *Several Arduous Matters under the Inspection of our House*. Go on.

TOM.   Wherefore it is our humble and earnest Supplication, That we may be once more put under your *Wild Distraction*.

FIZLE.   Mild Direction.

TOM.   Or that of the *Excrement Androboros*.

FIZLE.   Excellent *Androboros*.

TOM.   That so we may give a *Loose to Our Knavery*.

FIZLE.   I'm afraid, Sirrah, you are a Knave; Get loose from our Slavery.

TOM.   I'm afraid, Sirrah, you are a Knave; Get loose from our Slavery, and fix a *stolid Security for our Nasty Foundations*.

FIZLE.   Is the Dev'l in thee! A solid Foundation for our lasting Security.

TOM.   A solid Foundation for our lasting Security. And your Petitioners, *like Asses as they are, in a durty Pound,* shall never cease to *Bray*.

FIZLE.   (Raskal! it should be) like as they are in *Duty Bound, shall never cease to pray*. (I could swear he reads thus on purpose.)

ÆSOP.   And not be For-sworn. But have you done?

TOM.   Yes, an't please your Honors.

FIZLE.   Gentlemen, do you approve of this Draught?

ÆSOP.   I like it as the Clerk read it.

MULLIGRUB.   I approve of all, except the *Ordure;* I'll have it a T——:

COXCOM.   You'll have it a T——, A T—— in your Teeth; it shall stand as it is *Ordure*.

MULLIGRUB.   T——d.

DOODLESACK.   Ick been on the Cant van de t——d.

BABILARD.   Let us Compromise the Matter, and make it *Turdure*.

ALL.   Ay, agreed.

ÆSOP.   Gentlemen, you have agreed to the Draught of an Address; but what is to be done with it?

COXCOM.   Transmitted to *Oinobaros*.

ÆSOP.   For what purpose?

COXCOMB.   To get Rid of our Keeper, and get *Oinobaros* in his room.

ÆSOP.   If you should, my mind Forbodes you would repent the Change.

COXCOMB.   Why?

ÆSOP.   Why! why because a man who could never yet Govern himself, will make but a sorry Governor for others.

COXCOMB.   Have a care what you say; That is *Scandalum Magnatum*.

DOODLESACK. Pray, *Mr. Tom*. Wat is dat Lating? Ick forestae't niet.

TOM. He say, my Lord is in a very great Post, call'd *The Scandalum Magnatum*.

DOODLESACK. Is it given him lately.

TOM. No, he has it by inheritance.

ÆSOP. Be advis'd by me; Lay your Address aside, and keep as you are; As for your Keeper, none of you can say that he has done you any harm; and for my part I am convinc'd, that he has done us much good. I must beg leave to tell you a Story.

COXCOMB. Hang you and your Storys; we shan't mind 'em.

ÆSOP. You may give it the same fair play you did to *Mulligrub's* Speech; hear it, tho' you do not mind it. I pray your patience.

> The Frogs, a Factious fickle Race,
> With little Maners, and less Grace,
>   Croak'd for a King so loud,
> That all the Host of Heav'n sate mute
> Nodding to *Jove* to grant their suit,
>   And give 'em what they wou'd.
>
> A King they had, of such a size
> Who's Entry too, made such a Noise,
>   That Ev'ry Neut and Frog
> Affrighted, run to hide their heads;
> Some in the Pool, some 'mongst the Reeds,
>   Like Fools, 'Twas but a Log.
>
> At last, one bolder than the rest,
> Approach'd, and the new Prince Address't,
>   No hurt from thence sustain'd,
> He mock'd his former Fears, and swore
> 'Twas the best stick of Wood that o'er
>   The Marshes ever Reign'd.
>
> Then all the Croaking Crew drew near,
> And in his shade from th' angry Air
>   Were shelter'd safe, and eas'd,
> Nay, more then that, they'd frisk and play
> Upon his back a live long day,
>   He Undisturb'd and pleas'd.

The Pertest Frog of all the Pack,
A Toad, some say, his hue was Black;
 'Tis true; but that's no matter,
Upon the passive Monarch's head,
At times would Noxious Venom shed,
 And both his sides bespatter.

'Twas That same Frog, the Legends tell,
Burst when he only meant to swell,
 Soon after these Events.
Be that as 'twill, 'twas He that drew
That giddy Senseless Crowd to new
 Sedition and Complaints.

Give us a bustling King, *Dread Sir!*
They cry'd, a King that makes a stir;
 This is not to be mov'd.
Jove heard and gave 'm one, who's care
Was, that they should Obey and Fear,
 No matter how they Lov'd.

It was a *Stork,* who's Law-less Rage
Spar'd neither Sex, Degree nor Age,
 That came within his reach.
And that was great, for whilst his Claws
Ransack't the Deep, his Vulturs Jaws
 Could wander o'er the Beach.

Then they Implor'd the God to send
From heav'n a Plague, from Hell a Fiend,
 Or any but this Curse.
Peace, cry'd the Monarch of the Gods,
Ye Worms; Keep him you have, 'tis odds
 The Next may prove a Worse.

Now If you please, you may put the Question about your Address. I take it
to be Log or Stork. [*Enter Door-Keeper*]
 Door-Keeper. Here's a Courier from *Androboros,* just return'd from the
Expedition, who desires Admittance.

ÆSOP. It is the most Expeditious Expedition I ever heard of; let us adjourn the Address, and receive the General's Message.

FIZLE. Let him come in. [*Enter Messenger*]

MESSENGER. The Renown'd *Androboros* with a tender of his hearty Zeal and Affection sends this to the *Consistory,* the Senate being Discontinued. [*Delivers a Letter*]

FIZLE. [*Reads*] Right Frightful and Formidable, We Greet you Well, And by this Acquaint you, That for many Weighty Considerations Us thereunto moving, We have thought fit to adjourn the Indended Expedition to a more proper season, because we have, upon due and Mature Examination been fully convinc'd, that the *Mulomachians,* our Reputed Enemies, are in very deed our good and faithful Friends and Allies, who, to remove all Doubts and Scruples, have freely offer'd to Consolidate Consistories with us, as also to divide with us the Commerce of the World, generously resigning and yielding to us that of the two Poles, reserving to themselves only what may lie between e'm. They have likewise Condescended that we shall keep some Forts and Holds, which by the Fortune of the War they could not take from us, and have promis'd and engag'd to Raze and Demolish some Places in their Possession to our prejudice, so soon as more Convenient are built in their room and place. You are further to understand, to your Great satisfaction, that this is a Treaty Litteral and Spiritual, so that having two Handles it may be Executed with the greater Facility, or if need be, the One may Execute the other, and so it may Execute it self. Now these Concessions (tho' it be well known that I hate Boasting) having been obtain'd, in a great measure, by the Terror of my Name and Arms, I expect your Thanks. And so we bid you heartily *Farewell.*

Androboros.

ÆSOP. Buzzzzz, Hummmmm, Buzzzzz—

FIZLE. What Return shall we give to this Civil and Obliging Message?

ÆSOP. Return him his Letter.

COXCOMB. No, let us vote him Thanks, a Statue and a Triumph! [*Enter Keeper*]

KEEPER. Be not surpriz'd, I have heard what you are about, and Cordially joyn with you in what you propose, in honour of the Valiant *Androboros,* Having received instructions from my Superiors to use that mighty Man according to his Deserts.

ÆSOP. What! Is our Keeper Mad, too?

KEEPER. In the Mean time, all Retire to your respective Apartments, until due Dissposition be made for his Reception. [*Exit manent Fizle and Æsop*]

Scene IV:

Fizle. What Man! I'th Dumps, because our Keeper let fall a word or two about Orders to use a certain great Man according to his deserts!

Æsop. I hope he has receiv'd the same Orders relating to you.

Fizle. There is more in this than you Imagine; I ever believ'd, that it would come to this at last.

Æsop. Why? What's the matter?

Fizle. The Keeper undoubtedly has receiv'd Orders to resign to *Androboros*.

Æsop. What then?

Fizle. What then! I'll tell you what then; Then My Brethren and I shall have our due, and you with yours be proud to lick the Dust off our Feet.

Æsop. Ha'nt ye your Allowence?

Fizle. What of that? That's no more then the Law gives us.

Æsop. And you would have more. Law or Custom make an Inch to an Ell very fair allowance; you, it seems, want an Ell to an inch. I wish your Stint might be some how ascertain'd; but that, I doubt, cannot easily be compass'd. And whosoever, by giving hopes to find an end of your Craving will find himself deceiv'd, I'll tell you a Tale to this [Line missing]

> The Rats, a Tribe much better fed
>   Then taught, that mortally abhor'd
> To work, lov'd ease and eating, fled
>   For shelter to a *Saxon* Lord,
>   Who's Barns and Paunch were ever full,
>   And nothing Emply but his Skull.
>
> Here they did Revel at their ease,
>   Far from the watchful Pusses Eye;
> For he had banish't all that Race
>   For th' Love they bore to liberty
>   And Cleanliness, Things to his Nature
>   As opposite as Fire to Water.
>
> His steward put him oft in mind,
>   That all his plenty only serv'd
> To Fatten Vermin, whilst the Hind
>   That Labour'd, and his Servants starv'd;
>   And what was worse, th' Infirm and Poor
>   Unfed, Unpity'd, ply'd his Door.

To this, the Churle reply'd at length,
  And they may all starve on for me,
The Rats eat not above a Tenth,
    These would Consume me one in Three,
      They are the Rats that would destroy me,
      The other cannot much annoy me.

The pamper'd Tribe familiar grown
  By this Indulgence, Lodg'd themselves
No more as heretofore they ad done,
    In holes and Corners, and on Shelves,
      But in his Robes, and in the upshot,
      They ate his very Heart and Guts out.

God beyt't ye. [*Exit Æsop*]

  Fizle.   Rats! a Dog! I'll Rat ye, ye Whorson Tale—Teller, you Vermin! a Son of a Whore—[*Exit Fizle*]

ACT III.

Deputy. With all due Submission, Sir, give me leave to ask you what you mean by the splendid Reception you have promis'd to give to that Odd Man?

Keeper. Very little besides Diversion. My Superiors, as I am inform'd, have Cloath'd him with Sham-Powers meerly to get rid of his Noise and Trouble; and since these must fall to my share, I'll humour him to keep him quiet.

Deputy. That is not to be hop'd for whilst he lives.

Tom. Persuade him that he is dead then.

Keeper and Deputy. Ha, Ha, Ha,

Tom. It is far from Impossible, however Extravagant you may think the Overture. If you'll be rul'd by me, I'll answer for the Success of what I propose, under any Penalties you please. I'm sure he has had the Art to Dream himself into Notions every whit as Absurd. His Imagination is very ductile when 'tis heated, and by a Long Practice upon't, he has made it as susceptible of Impressions from Without, as it has been of these from Within. Do you but when he appears, behave your selves as if he were Invisible, and take no maner of Notice of what he shall say or do, and I'll answer for the rest. Here he comes, mind him not. [*Enter Androboros*]

Tom. I was not present, *Sir,* when he Expir'd, but arriv'd a few Minutes after.

Keeper. So suddenly too! I wish he may not have had foul play.

Androb. Your Servant, Gentlemen, I hope I do not Interrupt you; pray, who is it you speak of?

Tom. No, Sir, he dy'd of an uncommon Disease, The Physitians call it, a *Tympany in the Imagination,* occasion'd by a collection of much Indigested Matter there, which for the want of due Excretion, made a breach in the Pericrane, at which that great Soul took its flight.

Keeper. Had he made his Will?

Androboros. Pray, Gentlemen, who is it that's Dead?

Tom. I have not heard of any.

Androb. Cry mercy, I thought—

Tom. Only about the time he Expir'd, he Cry'd, I leave This World, this Worthless World to My Delamya, O Delamya!

ANDROB.   You Impudent Dog you, dare but to Profane that sacred Name with thy base breath, and I'll crush thee to Nothing.

TOM.   Hark, did you not hear an odd Noise?

DEPUTY.   Something like the Humming of a Bee.

TOM.   Me thinks it sounded rather like the Breath of the Bung of an Empty Barrel.

ANDROB.   You Sawcy Knave, Take that. [*Strikes him a Box o'th' Ear*]

TOM.   It was nothing but a Flea in my Ear. [*Scratching his Ear*] And so, (as I was saying,) with that Name in his Mouth he Expir'd.

ANDROB.   Gentlemen, I am not to be made a May-Game, your betters shall be acquainted with your Conduct. [*Exit*]

KEEPER.   Run, *Tom,* and allay or baulk his Fury. [*Exit Tom*] What d'ye think of Tom's Project, is it Not an Odd One?

DEPUTY.   I hardly believe He'll succeed, but if he does, what then!

KEEPER.   Then We shall live at ease, he'll dream no more, when he thinks that he's dead. It is amazing that this Mans Visions, like Yawning, should be catching. The Inhabitants of this Tenement are not the only Dupes of his *Quixotism.*

DEPUTY.   That Indeed is matter of Wonder; and if the Countenance given to Folly be not all Grimace, The World is as Mad as he. [*Enter Tom*]

TOM.   I have Instructed the Porter, and the other Servants, and have proclaim'd to all, the General remains *Incognito,* until he makes his Publick Entry, and that no notice is to be taken of him, more then if he were Absent, under the Pain of his highest Displeasure.

KEEPER.   So far all goes well. But you must Intrust *Solemn* and *Æsop* with your Plot.

TOM.   I have already. The first is to be my Conjurer.

KEEPER.   Conjurer!

TOM.   Yes, my Conjurer; To him alone, and that too but some times, he shall be visible, to all besides, a shadow, an Empty Name. Here they come. [*Enter Solemn and Æsop*]

KEEPER.   Gentlemen, you have your Q.

SOLEMN.   Do you but keep your Countenance, leave the rest to us. [*Chairs and a Table; they sit down. Enter Androboros*]

ANDROB.   Sure all the World is Mad, or have a mind to make me so; I try'd to get out, but the Porter lean't his Staff against my Nose, and belch't full in my Chops; a Culverine could not have done more suddain Execution than that Erruption of Barm and Tobacco Smoak.

SOLEMN.   When is he to be Interr'd?

TOM. This Ev'ning, but is to lie in State here till then.

ANDROBOROS. I made a Shift to recover my self, and attempted the back passage; but in the Door of the Kitchin I was saluted with a Pale of foul⁵ Water, which had like to have been succeeded by a Shovel of burning Coals, but that I made a speedy Retreat. Something's the matter, what e'er it is; I'll listen here and find it out.

KEEPER. But why so suddainly? 'Tis strange so Great a Man should be bury'd with so little Ceremony.

ANDROB. Bury'd, said he!

TOM. It is done by the advice of Physitians, who have declar'd that his Disease was such as makes a man stink vilely after he is dead.

KEEPER. The fair *Delamya!* how does she bear the loss?

TOM. She's Inconsolable, ready to burst her sides.

KEEPER. How! *Tom?* Yes, Sir, Excess of Joy makes some People Weep; Excess of Grief makes her Laugh Inordinately, and Cry out Incessantly, *Are these our promised Joys, O Androboros! One Grave shall hold us.* And then she laughs again.

ANDROB. *Androboros,* it seems then I'm dead; 'tis odd that I should not know it. I'll try that. [*Takes a Chair*]

KEEPER. Poor Lady, she lov'd him well, I doubt she'll be as good as her Word.

ÆSOP. Who set this Empty Chair by me?

SOLEMN. Save me, ye Kinder Powers, and guard my Senses!

KEEPER. What's the matter, Man? What d'ye see?

TOM. It is but a Raving fit, the Effect of deep study; he is often taken so.

SOLEMN. No, my sense is temperate as yours. Look there, There ☞

ÆSOP. There is a Chair, What then? [*Shoveing it with his foot*]

SOLEMN. Have ye no Eyes? Can't you see?

KEEPER. For my part I see nothing but what I use to see.

SOLEMN. Why there, in that Chair sits the Venerable Form of the deceas'd *Androboros,* in nothing differing from that Awful Figure he once made, but that you regard it not.

KEEPER. Sure he Raves.

ÆSOP. That Chair. Why there's nothing in that Chair. There it lies. [*Strikes down Androboros, Chair and all*]

SOLEMN. O! Offer it no Violence.

ANDROB. You Old Dog, I'll be Reveng'd. [*Goes off*]

SOLEMN. See how it Stalks off! With what Majestick Air, and how Stern a Brow! It Resents the Indignity offer'd. Ha, Ha, Ha.

ALL. Ha, Ha, Ha, Ha.

Tom. Now we have him; it begins to work, if I do not mistake his Looks.

Deputy. I had much ado to contain my self.

Keeper. What's next to be done?

Tom. Trust that to me; but be sure not to mind him, ev'n tho' he should be Outragious. To *Solemn* only he must be visible for some time. Have you got your Conjuring Tackle ready?

Solemn. I have, That will serve the turn. O here he comes again in very pensive Mood and doleful Dumps. All walk off, as if you saw him not; I'll remain alone. [*Exeunt Keeper, Deputy, Tom and Æsop, passing by Androboros without taking Notice of him*]

Scene II: *Solemn at the Table with Books and Implements. Enter Androboros.*

Androb. 'Tis Strange, Wondrous strange, I should take the whole to be a Trick, were it not that my best, my firmest Friends, who never could be Induc'd to practice upon me in this gross manner, behave themselves to my Face as if they saw me not. Whilst I sate at the Table, That only Raskal, *Solemn* saw me, and started and star'd as if he had seen a Ghost; The rest saw nothing. They were talking of my Disease, Death, Burial and latter Will, as of things certain, and of publick knowledge. I think I'm pretty sure that I am Alive, tho' it seems, I am singular in that belief. I See, I Feel, I Hear as I us'd to do, ev'n now I hear my own Voice as plain as can be; I have Thought and Reflection as usual. But, Alas! departed Spirits if they think at all, must think that they do think, that is, that they are not dead,—It may be so—Ev'n that very Knave who but now could see me, sits musing by himself as if I were not here. I Remember it was the Common Opinion that a Ghost that walks, could be seen but by One of a Company. But why should he be blind now? [*Walks nearer*]

Solemn. It must Portend some suddain Change i 'th' State; For Ghosts of Note never walk but upon these solemn Errands.

Androb. He does not see me yet; I remember I was on th' other side when he saw me last. [*Goes to the other side*]

Solemn. If the poor Spirit is permitted once more to haunt these Walls, I'll question it, if my Courage fail me not; he may, perhaps, have something of Moment in Commission.

Androb. If you can't see me, can't you hear me, you old Dev'l you? [*Bawling*]

Solemn. How painful, yet unprofitable are all the deeper ways of Art? The Vulgar undisturb'd, Frequent the silent Shades, and quietly enjoy the pleasure of soft Recess or Balmy Slumbers, whilst I whom Science has rais'd so far above them, have not a peaceful hour. If at any time I would see into Futurity, I must take my *Talisman,* and then all Ghosts or Spectres which chance at that time to crowd the Ambient Air, become visible to me, and to me alone. Not dreaming of any search into the Intellectual World; but by meer Chance, I grasp'd my *Talisman* thus, when streight— [*Takes a Tobacco-stopper out of his Pocket. Starts up Wildly*]

Angels and all the Ministers of Grace, Defend me. Be thou a Spirit of Health, or Goblin Damn'd! Bring with thee Airs from Heav'n, or Blasts from Hell, Thou Com'st in such a Questionable Shape, I'll speak to Thee. Thanks Good Hamlet for this again, I'll [*Softly*] call thee General. Valiant *Androboros,* O speak.

ANDROB.   I tell you, ye Old Fool—

SOLEMN.   O speak, if ought of dire Import.

ANDROB.   Why, I'll tell you, Sirrah—

SOLEMN.   To this our state disturbs thy sacred Shade, impart, O speak.

ANDROB.   Let me speak then, and be hang'd—

SOLEMN.   For sure no common Cause could raise thee from thy silent Herse.

ANDROB.   'Owns! Can your Talisman make you See, and not make you Hear, You Old Conj'ring *Dog,* you?

SOLEMN.   Its Lips Tremble, as if it would Speak, but this is not the time. Up, Up, my *Talisman,* and give thy Master and the Perturbed Spirit Quiet for a Season.— [*Puts Up his Tobacco-stopper*] Now all is well again.— [*Sits down*] Sure something is Amiss, what-e'er it is.

ANDROB.   Now he has lost Sight of Me again. Take out your what d'ye-call't once more, and may be I may tell you all.

SOLEMN.   If I should impart this Odd Event to others, they'll not Credit it, and to show him in his Aerial Form, I dare not.

ANDROB.   Can you show me to other Folks? I'm glad of that. You shall—

SOLEMN.   Lest the Odious Name of Conjurer should be fixt upon me, and I (such is the prevailing Ignorance and Envy of the Age) instead of being Reverenc'd for my Science be hang'd for a Wizzard.

ANDROB.   Look ye, I'll answer for you.

SOLEMN.   Some other time I'll venture further, Mean while 'tis fit that I retire and ruminate upon this odd Phœnomenon, and find out by my *Talismanick Art* some means to unsear its Lips. [*Exit*]

ANDROB.   Unsear your Ears, ye Old Buzzard, I can speak, but you, it seems, can't hear. He's gone, a Pestilence go with him. I can't tell what to think of it; Am I bew'itch't, or am I really Dead, as they say? It cannot be.

Why, is not that a Hand as plain as a Pike Staff? Is not this a Nose? Don't I feel? Yes surely, to my Cost; for my back Akes still with the bruise I got when that Villain *Æsop* Over-set my Chair—yet I remember to have heard the learned say, that it is the Soul alone that Feels, the Body is but a Senseless Mass. If I did not think, I should not feel; then Perhaps I only think I feel. Think! I know not what to think, or whether I think at all, If I am Alive or Dead, or whether I ever was alive or no. Sure all this cannot be a Dream; I wish it were, and that I were fairly awake. O here come my good Friends, *Fizle* and *Flip*. Now I shall know. [*Enter Fizle and Flip*]

FIZLE. You must take no Notice of him at all, before he makes his Publick Entry; He'll have it so, and you know his Humor. Poor *Tom* has been Whipt almost to Death by his Orders, for barely Saluting him.

FLIP. That is a little Whimsical, by the by; me thinks he might be visible to his Friends.

ANDROB. What's that? Pray Gentlemen, let me ask you one Question, because I hear, That there is some Doubt [of] my Visibility; D'ye see me? Am I Alive or Dead? What d'ye think?

FIZLE. I told you so, this he does to try our Obedience. Answer him Not.

ANDROB. Will neither of you Answer me?

FIZLE. At six a Clock I'll meet you here again. Adue. [*Exeunt severally, without Noticing him*]

ANDROB. They're Gone, and saw me not! Nay, then 'tis too True, I am Dead, as sure as I'm Alive; Dead, Dead as a Herring, and something worse too; for I am Condemn'd to Converse with no Body, but Old *Solemn,* who ever was a Hell upon Earth to me. Would I could change that Doom for any other. Could I but have the Company of my Fellow Ghosts, I should be in some measure Happy, but that is not my Lot, it seems. If the Old Conjurer can but unsear Lips, as he calls it, or uncork his own Ears, as I take it, I might perhaps prevail with him to Conjure me a little better Conversation than his own. It is Tormenting, that I must be oblig'd to him: but there is no Remedy; I'll Wheadle him with a Story of the other World, of which I know as little as he does; That may work upon him. [*Enter Tom with a Broom Sweeping the Gallery*]

TOM. What a Clutter is here about the Earthing an Old Stinking Corps; Would he had Lain in State in some other place; but rest his Soul, such was his Will. [*Sings*]

> *Whenas* Old Nick-Nack *Rul'd this Land,*
> *A Doughty Blade he wore.*
> *Four Dozen dragons Hides he Tann'd,*
> *Of Gyants eke Four Score.*

Androb. I wonder if the Ghosts of other Men hear all the Vile Things that are said and Sung of them after their Death? [*Tom sweeps the Dust on him*]

Tom. *But now he's Dead, and laid in Clay.*—This Dust most Abominably Salt, I must qualify't a little. [*Drinks, and spurts it upon him*] What a Plaguy Earthy Taste this same small Beer has got, all of a suddain. [*Sings*]

    But now he's Dead and laid in Clay,—

Androb. That's a Lye, for I a'n't Bury'd yet, by his own Confession.
Tom.
      Alack, and Wo therefore,
    The Gyants they may go to play,
    The Dragons sleep and snore.

What a Carrion stink there is; the more I sweep the more it stinks.

Androb. *Solemn* Can see me, but can't hear me; This Fellow can neither see me nor hear me; but he can smell me; I'll try if he can feel me.

Tom. *The Dragons sleep and snore.*—The stink Comes that way. [*Buts him on the Breast with the Broom*] I'll perfume the Air a little. [*Besprinkles him with the Bottle*]

Androb. Hold, Sirrah, hold. Well, if I were alive they durst not have us'd me thus; This Usage convinces me more then any thing else. [*Exit*]

Tom. He has it, he has it; I doubt it will be a hard matter to persuade him to Life again.

Scene III: *Enter Fizle and Flip.*

Fizle. We see, *Tom,* you are very busy. But if it be no Interruption, pray give us leave to ask you, In what manner the General is to make his Entry?

Tom. You have it.

Fizle. Nay, Answer us Directly.

Tom. I do, you have Leave.

Flip. Well then, In what manner is the General to make his Entry?

Tom. Ask him.

Fizle. Thank you for that; Ask him, and have our Curiosity answer'd as was yours. But we know that it depends in a great measure on the Keeper, and you of late are more in his Confidence than we.

Tom. If it depends upon the Keeper, He'll make his Entry by way of Exit? If upon himself, it is Problematical, and admits of several Solutions.

Flip. As how?

Tom. Either, *Hurry-Durry, Hum-Drum,* or *Blud and 'Owns.* Rest you Merry, Gentlemen. [*Exit*]

Fizle. We shall learn nothing from this Fellow; but so far we know, that the Keeper must assist at it; And from a broad by hints we have understood, that if he is destroy'd any how, so the General be not seen in't, He'll take that Trust upon himself; Then all will be Well. Now if we can but Contrive to have the Chair over Loaded, plac'd Upon the Hatch over the Vault, and the Hatch Unbolted, or so weakly Barr'd, that its weight may sink him Down, we shall get Rid of him, and it will appear to the world to be the meer Effect of Chance.

Tom. [*Peeping*] Are you there with your Bears? I shall be up with you. I'll go find out *Solemn,* and try to build on this Foundation of their own Laying. [*Exit*]

Flip. This is Admirable, and cannot fail; Let's loose no time, but go about it streight; I'll get into the Vault, and Prepare the Bolt; do you take care to place the Chair. Here comes old *Solemn;* no more words, but *Mumm.* [*Exeunt. Enter Solemn and Tom*]

Solemn. Are you sure that you heard distinctly? The Excess of the Villainy makes it incredible!

Tom. Am I sure that I live? But if you doubt it, the very Tampering with the Chair will Convince you.

Solemn. Away then, acquaint the Keeper, and *Æsop,* leave the rest to me. One thing you must take care be Punctually Observ'd, that is, That *Androboros* Friends be planted next to the Chair, by way of Precedency. Quick, Quick, be gone.

Tom. I fly. [*Exit*]

Solemn. When Malice becomes a Moral Virtue, that Couple must be sainted; if the Long Robes were made use of only to Cover the Personal Defects and Blemishes of those who wear 'em, much might be said in their Defence; but when they are worn or lent to Cover Daggers, and Poyson prepar'd for the Innocent, is there a Mortal so devoid of Humanity as to appear on their side? If, as the Philosophers speak, the Corruption of the best Things produces the Worst, the Abuse of Things Sacred must he [be] Dev'lish. O! you are come in good time. [*Enter Æsop*] Pray get all in order for this same Entry; Neglect not that part of the Ranking them, which I, by *Tom,* recommended to you. I'll Equip the General, and dispose him for his Triumph: In the mean while do you Intertain 'em with a Tale, or how you please, until he comes.

Æsop. Dispatch then, for they grow Impatient. [*Exit Æsop. Enter Androboros*]

ANDROB. I hope he has by this time found a way to unsear my Lips or his own Ears, no matter which.

SOLEMN. Here he comes pat. *Nick-Nack,* How dos't do? I'm glad to see thee Awake with all my heart.

ANDROB. Is the Dev'l in the Fellow? He can see me now without the help of his Gymcrack; not to mention your odd Familiarity. What d'ye mean by Awake? When was I asleep?

SOLEMN. Asleep! You have been so Time out of mind. You have been Walking asleep, Talking asleep, and Fighting asleep, I know not how long.

ANDROB. I'm glad it's no Worse; I Thought I was Dead, at least every body else seem'd to think so.

SOLEMN. Dead! No, No; it is all a Jest.

ANDROB. Why, you old Raskal, you, Did not you but now start at the sight of me, as if you had seen a Ghost?

SOLEMN. True; yet you are not actually Dead, but Invisible to all the World besides, and must continue so, so long as I shall think fitting.

ANDROB. [*Aside*] I ever thought this Fellow had the black Art. [*To him*] I wish thou would'st change that Curse for any other. Canst thou not make thy self invisible to me, as thou hast done me to other Folks? So far I own I would be oblig'd to thee, and thank thee.

SOLEMN. If that will oblige you, 'tis done, Look but into this Telescope, and in that instant I shall become invisible to you. [*Looks into a hollow Cane; Solemn from the other End blows Snuff into his Eyes*] It is done?

ANDROB. Villain, Dog, Raskal, I'm blind; Where are ye, ye Villain. Murderer?

SOLEMN. Here, This way, This way; You must see with your Ears, until I shall think fit to unsear your Eyes, General; That is the bargain, if I remember right. [*Exit Solemn, Androb. Groping his way after him*]

SCENE IV: *Curtain drawn, Discovers Keeper, Deputy, Tom, Æsop, Fizle, Flip, Coxcomb, Babilard, Mullegrub, &c.*

KEEPER. Let the Black Gentlemen be Rank'd as they desire; I'll do all I can to please e'm.

ÆSOP. With all my Heart, Only I thought it bad Heraldry that these who are supported by the Chair, should support it.

KEEPER. Another time you shall have your way; I'll have it so now; Let the Rest observe their distance. [*Here they are rank'd, Fizle and Flip next to the Chair*]

ÆSOP. I'll keep as distant as I can, that I may be at Ease; *Fizle's* Phiz always gives me the Chollick. I know not why he should be suffer'd to walk at Large, to the Detriment of his Majestys Leige People, whilst so many of his Species up and down the World are Insty'd, Inkennel'd, Impounded or Incloyster'd. Did you ever hear how that came about? I'll tell you, If you please.

KEEPER. Come on.

ÆSOP.   And First of the First.

> Nature, which nothing leaves to Chance,
>   Had dealt to Creatures of each Kind,
> Provision for their Sustenance,
>   To some her Bounty had Assign'd
>   The Herb o'th' Fields, whilst others had
>   The Spoils of Trees, but All were Fed.
>
> The Grunting Kind obtain'd the last,
>   A happy Lot; for every Wood
> Afforded store of Nuts and Mast,
>   And *Joves* own Tree did Show'r down Food
>   Enough for all, could all his Store
>   Have kept that Herd from Craving more.
>
> But they with Sloath and Plenty Cloy'd,
>   Wax'd Wanton, and with Tusks Profane,
> First, all the sacred Trees Destroy'd,
>   Which fed 'em; Next invade the Plain,
>   Where harmless Flocks did graze, and Spoil
>   With Rav'nous Snouts the fertile Soil.
>
> *Jove* hears the loud Complaints and Cry's
>   Of Suff'ring Flocks, and streight Ordains,
> That hence-forth Hogs be pen't in Sty's,
>   And fed with Wash, and Husks, and Grains,
>   Where ever since th' Unhallow'd Race
>   Wallows in Fat and Filthyness.

Secondly, Beloved—

KEEPER. No, No, We have enough of the first. [*Noise within*] What Noise is that?

ANDROB. [*Within*] I'll have the Villain Hang'd; Dog, Raskal, Rogue, Scoundrel.

ÆSOP. By my Life, it is the General making his Entry; It seems he has got no Herald for this Triumph, that he thus Proclaims his own Titles. [*Enter Solemn, Androboros following him*]

SOLEMN. Make way there, Make way; Room, Room for the General. This Way,—This Way— [*Solemn Steps aside, Androboros Runs blindly upon the Chair, Fizle and Flip Endeavouring to Stop him, Sink with Him*]

FIZLE and FLIP. Hold, Hold; Help! Help! Help!

KEEPER. What's the meaning of this?

SOLEMN. 'Tis but a Trap of their Own laid for you, Sir, in which They Themselves are Caught.

COXCOMB. Let's be gone! There is no Safety here. [*Coxcom. Babilard, Mulligrub Sneaking off*]

SOLEMN. What! You are making your Retreat; you need not fear, you are a sort of Vermin not worth the Bait; The others have their Deserts.

In former Ages virtuous Deeds
 Rais'd Mortals to the blest Abodes,
But Hero's of the Mode[r]n Breed
 And Saints go downward to the Gods.

         [*Exeunt*]

     Curtain Falls.

     FINIS.

NOTES

1. Reference to a true incident. See Gov. Hunter's proclamation on March 3, 1713/14.
2. "Please" was changed to "feed" by Gov. Hunter.
3. Edward Hyde, Viscount Cornbury and Earl of Clarendon (1661–1723).
4. William Dockwra.
5. "Cold" was changed to "foul" by Gov. Hunter.

THE TRIAL OF ATTICUS

BEFORE JUSTICE BEAU, FOR A RAPE

Since none the living villains dare implead,
Arraign them in the persons of the dead.

Dryden's *Juvenal*

BOSTON:

Printed and sold by ISAIAH THOMAS, near the Mill-Bridge,
for the Author. MDCCLXXI.

To The

Most Honourable, Most Worshipful

and Most Worthy

JOSIAH BEAU, Esq;

COLONEL of a REGIMENT of FOOT, JUSTICE of the PEACE, and of the QUORUM, for the County of————.

Great Sir,

As the compiling the following Trial, was designed to transmit to posterity, some of the many excellent qualifications, with which you are so distinguishly endowed above the rest of mankind, particularly, in your *magistratical* character; and as the case I have chosen from among many others, was one, that called on your Worship, to exercise those noble talents, with which you are so richly blessed: I could think of no fitter person to dedicate this attempt to, than your RIGHT WORSHIPFUL SELF, to whom it is with the most profound veneration inscribed; by

Your Worship's
most obedient
humble Servant,
The COMPILER.

TO THE READER

IT is the common method of original authors, first, to dedicate their performances to some great man, whose aid and patronage they most humbly and devoutly implore; secondly, by way of preface, to apologize with their readers, for intruding on the public, imperfections and deficiencies in matter, stile, &c.

It certainly then does not become a Compiler, to be too assuming, but to follow their foot steps.

Here then by way of preface, I would say, that as to a Patron, I am safe as I can wish; for apology, I would say, that I thought a case, (especially as it was managed by two such able hands) so interwoven, so critical, and so interesting; must be of great utility to Justices, Lawyers, Complainants, Evidences, Doctors, Conjurers, Innholders and Deacons.

The Compiler has added nothing of his own, but only given a plain narration of facts, as they were delivered by each party, whom we shall describe by the following names, viz.

COL. JOSIAH BEAU, Justice of the Peace.
EZEKIEL CHUCKLE, and ⎱ *Com-*
MRS. CHUCKLE, his wife. ⎰ *plainants.*
MR. RATTLE, a Lawyer.
WILLIAM FROTH, a Conjurer.
DEACON GRISSEL, friend to CHUCKLE; DR. PIP, LIEUTENANT NATHANIEL SCANT, JOHN FOX, MRS. PRIM, CAPTAIN TIMON, PAUL SHEPARD, AZARIAH BLUSTER, and CAESAR, *Witnesses at the Trial.*

A Parlour in the Justice's House in B———e. Enter Chuckle, bowing and scrapping.

JUSTICE. Good morning, Sir, what important business has brought you here at this early hour of the day? If I might guess, Sir, by your eager, melancholy, pensive look, it is something of consequence. Does it regard the peace of the King, Sir? Of that, as being one of his Majesty's Justices of the Peace, and of the Quorum too, Sir, I have a special care. You cannot therefore, I trust, take my enquiring any way amiss; for magistrates ought always to be vigilant, to discover and punish vice, and reward virtue.

CHUCKLE. What the *Curnal* has said is well enough for that matter; I came *a* purpose to complain to you about something that I can't, nor won't, bear.

JUSTICE. Is it a breach of the common peace, Sir?

CHUCKLE. I don't know about the peace; but I know I have been abused, and my wife more than I.—A fellow came—

JUSTICE. I must interrupt you—let me understand as you go along,—your wife and you injured!—by whom and how? but hold, I had better put on my gown, and go into the office. [*They go into the office*] I shall now take your examination under oath, you may else casually drop a word that will expose you; but if you are sworn you will have no reason to fear; for any thing you will have occasion to say, Sir, the adverse party cannot take hold of.

CHUCKLE. I am obliged to the *Curnal* for this advice, for I am afraid I cannot prove all I would say,—if my oath will answer, I will swear in a minute. [*Enter Mrs. Chuckle*] Here's my wife too,—mayn't she swear? She knows more about the matter than I do,—I don't believe she has told me one half.

JUSTICE. Your request is highly reasonable, that your wife's deposition should be taken as well as your's, as it seems the matter concerns her as well as you,—is that your wife, Sir?

CHUCKLE. Yes, that's she.

JUSTICE. How do you do, Ma'am?—please to stand up,—oaths *of this nature* must be *taken standing,*—but stay a little,—you may sit down again, —there is something new comes into my mind, that possibly will do better. —If my memory is not treacherous, you said, Sir, [*Turning to Mr. Chuckle*] you was afraid your proof was not sufficient.

CHUCKLE. No, Sir, I only said I wanted to say more than I could prove.

JUSTICE. It amounts to the same thing, Sir,—you had as good give me some general hints of the case, and of the person, and I will write to him, possibly it will so *terrify* him, as to make him give you *satisfaction,*—and if so, take a *sufficiency* to *compensate* for *my trouble.* If it has not this effect, it may have a still better,—he may come in person to see me, and in his trying to get favour from me, I shall catch him myself, but whether I can, or cannot, I can speak without any danger, for no oaths are required of me, which is a privilege that gentlemen of my commission have above common men; and in cases circumstanced, as I guess your's is, it is highly beneficial.— [*Turning to Mrs. Chuckle*] Please give me a hint or two, Ma'am.

MRS. CHUCKLE. Why, Sir, one *Atticus* came to the house, and asked me to set down on the bed with him, but I had my children in my arms, and could not, then he—

JUSTICE. Hold Ma'am, you need not proceed any further,—I understand the matter,—surely he was a villain.—Pray how long ago was this, Ma'am?

MRS. CHUCKLE. About two years.

JUSTICE. Two years, Ma'am! How came you to defer the matter so long?

CHUCKLE. Why,—my wife and I did not love to make a noise about it, and so let it alone, from time to time, till my wife whispered it to one of our neighbours, and *Atticus* heard it, and threatened to prosecute me.

JUSTICE. Abusive villain, did he?

CHUCKLE. Yes, he did, and then I was advised to come down to you, to save myself; for I was told, that if he prosecuted first, our oaths would not be taken.

JUSTICE. They might have passed,—I cannot say they would have been quite so good, Sir,—the method you have taken is certainly the best, for now you have the whip-row of him, as the Lawyers sometime express it.—Can you recollect the day, Ma'am?

MRS. CHUCKLE. I did not *lay it up,* at first, and now I can't remember it.

JUSTICE. You must tell as near as you can,—you are not on oath you remember.

MRS. CHUCKLE. It was sometime between the middle of July, and the last of August,— [*Turning to Chuckle*] *wan't* it *Chuckle?*—I told you of it about a fortnight after.

CHUCKLE. Why, I've forgot the day, too,—it was within the time my wife says.

JUSTICE. It is not material.—I will write, and you must do me the favour to give him the letter. [*Writes*] Mr. *Chuckle,* I will read you what I have wrote. I think it is well contrived to answer *our purpose,* it is as follows. [*Reads*]

Sir,

"It gives me the greatest pain, that any mortal can feel, that I am obliged to address you in the manner following.—There has, Sir, been complaint made to me as Justice of the Peace, by Mr. *Ezekiel Chuckle,* and *Sarah* his wife; that you in some fatal hour—fatal, I say, for I am afraid it will end so, did by force of arms, commit a rape on the body of the said *Sarah,* the proof against you is ample and absolute.—It is the real friendship and regard that I ever had for you, Sir, that has induced me to take this trouble.—I could as easily have sent an officer, with a warrant, as this letter. Pray, Sir, in all love to yourself settle the matter, this I would do, were I in your case, if it cost me my whole estate, which you know, Sir, is pretty large.—If you should chuse to come to me, and compromise the matter you may—for you are to know, Sir, that the King, and all crown officers, have a dispensing power, and if the King is made easy, who of his subjects durst complain,—but if you neglect my advice, and do not apply yourself, either to myself, or to the complainant, and make satisfaction, he will pursue you with vengeance, in which I shall assist him, as by a sacred oath I am bound to do.

I am, Sir, with great Respect,

Your humble servant,

B—t-ee, Aug. 30, 1770.   J. BEAU, *Jus. Pacis.*

[*To Mr.* ATTICUS.]

—And now, Mr. *Chuckle,* do not fail of being here with your wife to-morrow morning, and let me know what he says, and with what countenance he reads it,—and so your humble servant. My servant calls me to breakfast, besides it is the usual hour, which I never allow myself to pass. [*Exit Omnes*]

The Justice's House in B——e. Justice present. Enter Chuckle, and his Wife.

CHUCKLE. Good morning, *Curnal,* if you have eat your breakfast, I am ready to tell you how that impudent fellow behaved when I gave him your letter.

JUSTICE. Behaved, Sir! was he not very thankful to me.

CHUCKLE. No, indeed, he was so far from that, that he flew into a passion, and swore.

JUSTICE. Swore, did you say, Sir?

CHUCKLE. Yes, Sir, but I could not hear one word he said; here's a letter he sent you. [*Justice takes the letter, reads the superscription*]

JUSTICE. How the superlatively unmannerly villain has superscribed it! it is only directed to *J. Beau,* Esq.

CHUCKLE. How should it be?

JUSTICE. Why, Sir, the superscription should have run thus, to Colonel *Josiah Beau,* Esq; the words all wrote at length; I'll read the letter to myself. [*Justice reads*] Mr. *Chuckle,* I have not the patience to go half way through; this *Atticus* is the most insolent brazen-fronted monster that I ever saw; instead of a handsome address, he attacks me in the following language,

"SIR,

"I KNOW nothing of the pretended crime you say *Chuckle* has charged me with, if he has the proof you are so sure of, I must submit to the punishment the law in such cases has provided, I shall make no private satisfaction.   Your's ATTICUS.

    "To J. Beau, *Esq;*"

Why really, Sir, if a poor Plebian in *Paris* (*Paris,* Sir, is the metropolis of France) was to write such a letter to a *Compte,* which is a title not more dignified there, than what I have the honour to sustain here, he would directly be put to the torture, *ordinary,* and *extraordinary,* and lastly be broken on the wheel as his just demerit; but in this country, Sir, a magistrate has little more respect shewn to him, than to a common man, which is highly abominable, and if things are not soon altered, we shall run into anarchy and confusion, but I will make an example of this villain.— [*Turns to Mrs. Chuckle*] Mrs. *Chuckle,* make your complaint on oath to me immediately— I'll grant a warrant, and have the wretch seized as soon as possible. [*Administers an oath to Mrs. Chuckle*] You are sworn Mrs. *Chuckle,* proceed. [*Turns to Mr. Chuckle*]—Mr. *Chuckle,* do bid my servant hand my gown,—I feel somewhat of a chill in my blood,—does the sun shine?—I have been so busy I've not had leisure to go abroad. [*To Mrs. Chuckle*] Well, Ma'am, I wait.

MRS. CHUCKLE. Why, Sir, he came,—

JUSTICE. You are wrong, Ma'am, you should not say *he* came, but *Atticus* came. You must be very explicit now.

MRS. CHUCKLE. Well, Sir, *Atticus* came to our house one day, about the hour I told you before, and asked if my husband was at home, I told him, no Sir; he then sits in my lap.

JUSTICE. Did not you endeavour to hinder him?

MRS. CHUCKLE. I had my sewing work in my hand, I cou'dn't, Sir,—then he put his hand on my knees—*your Honour knows what them be,* I suppose.

JUSTICE. Very well, Ma'am, proceed.

MRS. CHUCKLE. Why then he asked me to set on the bed.

JUSTICE. And did you, Ma'am?

MRS. CHUCKLE. Yes, Sir, and he too, and what he would have done I know not, if my child had not cried,—and I was obliged to go and take care of it.

JUSTICE. Did you cry out, Ma'am?

MRS. CHUCKLE. I should, Sir, but he said his head ached, and could not bear a noise.

JUSTICE. Very well, Ma'am, it is sufficient,—I'll make out a warrant,—but — [*Turns to Mr. Chuckle*] Mr. *Chuckle,* although I am a judge of law and justice, yet I am not versed in all points and niceties of law,—I should advise you to go to my kinsman, Lawyer *Rattle,*—but a few steps off,—whilst I am writing the warrant,—take his council, he will set you in the way to manage matters to all intents and purposes.

CHUCKLE. I am obliged to the *Curnal,* I think I'll do as you say; farewell, Sir.

JUSTICE. Your most humble.— [*Exit Chuckle and wife. Justice writes*]

Lawyer's house in B——e.

LAWYER. Servant, somebody knocks at the gate, let them in.— [*Enter Mr. Chuckle*] Your servant, Sir,—What's your business?

CHUCKLE. I'm sent by *Curnal Beau,* to ask your advice on a case that I have before him, against one *Atticus.*

LAWYER. It is very well, Sir; I'm greatly obliged to Mr. Justice *Beau,* for the honour he doth me;—Indeed, Sir, he had no right to give counsel in a case that was to come before him.

CHUCKLE. This *Atticus,* came one day to—

LAWYER. Not quite so fast, Sir,—I've got no fee.—It is direct in the face of the law to hear a case, or give advice without one; nay, it was known, that any gentleman of the law was to presume such a thing—the King's Attorney would immediately issue a warrant against him for barratry,—his punishment would be no less than the loss of both his ears.

CHUCKLE. How much must you have?

LAWYER. A guinea for the first hearing.

CHUCKLE. That's pretty dear, I think! but here it is, I don't care,—it is money given to me on purpose to carry on this prosecution, by some of my neighbours, that are disaffected to *Atticus.*

LAWYER. Given you, did you say? never mention that again: The law disallows any instigations of lawsuits by money or otherwise; but may be, their design was for you to procure my advice with it,—if so, there can lay no action either against you or them,—no more of this matter,—I've got the money,—proceed,—stay, let me first look into Coke and Littleton.[1] [*Takes down a book and mumbles to himself*]—Now, Sir, your case.

CHUCKLE. This *Atticus* tried to force my wife.

LAWYER. Was it against her will that he offered violence?

CHUCKLE. I never heard her say it was, but there is no doubt of it.

LAWYER. Granted, if it was force, it must be against her will, whether she say so or not.

CHUCKLE. He led her to the bed and both set down, and she verily believes he would have overcome her, if the child had not cried.

LAWYER. Enough, if this can be proved, you are as sure as you need wish for; and the villain will meet the just demerit of his wickedness. It matters not whether he did absolutely commit the fact, or not—the design is the thing, that will be considered and punished. I need say no more on this point now,—when I go before his honour, I shall expatiate more largely. Now as to the proof, Sir,—the proof is all—if he was *ipso facto,* to commit the rape, and there was no proof of it, you could not hang the dog. You are sensible of this, Mr. *Chuckle.*

CHUCKLE. My wife and I can swear to it, I think that is proof.

LAWYER. Granted, but did you, yourself, see the abuse he offered?

CHUCKLE. No; but she told me *on't* with her own mouth, about a fortnight after.

LAWYER. A fortnight after! you surprize me, why this circumstance will cut off your evidence, and that will leave but one. If she had complained to you immediately, it would have been a circumstance that would have amounted to positive evidence; which evidence is now wanting. You have not been so inadvertent I trust, as to give such a deposition before the Justice.

CHUCKLE. Yes I did.

LAWYER. Why the Devil's in you,—sho, sho, sho! I am heartily sorry; you should have come to me first,—I'd have told you better. Now it is too late.

CHUCKLE. I'm as sorry as you are, now I shall lose my guinea, and all, sha'nt I?

LAWYER. I hope not; there is one chance for you: What is his character? If any thing of this kind can be proved against him, we may still bring him to justice, and you recover your money, with other damages. When you come on trial, let his character stand as it will, you must renewedly take your oath; and it may so happen, that the circumstance I have mentioned, may have slipt the Justice's memory: Beware then how you speak, be positive your wife complained as soon as possible.

CHUCKLE. I'll take care now, I'll warrant you; but I don't question many things might be pick'd up against him; he has certainly a great many enemies; Mr. *William Froth* told me that—

LAWYER. Not so fast, Sir; who is this *Will. Froth?*

CHUCKLE. He is a man thirty-five years of age, who is now living with Dr. *Pip,* to learn to be a *Doctoror.* Folks say he is a conjurer, and can tell any thing he's a mind to; and that Dr. *Pip* was to swap skills with him.

LAWYER. What d'ye mean by that?

CHUCKLE. Why he was to learn Dr. *Pip* to conjure; and Dr. *Pip* was to learn him to *doctor.*

LAWYER. Pho, pho! Dr. *Pip* would disdain the name of conjurer, as much as he would of quack.

CHUCKLE. They don't call themselves conjurers, they have got a learn't word for it; I can't remember, but it was like—*stro—strolo—strolog—strolo-gers,* something, I don't know,

LAWYER. Astrologer, Sir, I guess is what you mean.

CHUCKLE. Yes, yes; that's the word.

LAWYER. Aye! if Mr. *Froth* be an astrologian, it's highly proper for you to consult him: If there is any misunderstanding between him and *Atticus,* I warrant ye, he'll not miss a figure, and a careful calculation will open all his misbehaviour; at the same time he tells you, who is most knowing to his wickedness.

CHUCKLE. Oh! I know he hates *Atticus* as bad as the Devil.

LAWYER. You had better apply yourself to him, before you take the warrant, that you may be able to tell the *Justice* the names of the witnesses.

CHUCKLE. Well, Sir, farewell. [*Exit*]

Froth's house. Enter Chuckle.

FROTH. Welcome, Mr. *Chuckle;* what's the news? how goes on affairs? have you got your warrant?

CHUCKLE. No; but I shall have it soon, for the *Curnal* and Lawyer are both well pleased with it.

FROTH. Have you been to a Lawyer then?

CHUCKLE. Yes; I have been to Lawyer *Rattle;* and he makes no doubt of my success, only there was one circumstance in my giving my oath, that should have been otherwise: He's afraid it will make some trouble, but has thought of a method, he says, will set all to rights again; and that is to prove him a man of bad character; and now you must study your *strologers* for your life, to find who can sware against him.

FROTH. Ah! I need not have asked you any questions, for I knew this

morning before sunrise, that you would need my advice, and I am prepared
to answer your requests; but for fear I have made a mistake, I'll consult my
books again; let me see, there is *Mars* and *Venus* in the ninth house, in
conjunction with *Saturn:* Oh! he's been a devilish fellow. Let me see further;
there is *Jupiter, Mercury* and the *Moon* in *Trine,* opposite the sun; you'll
easily prove him an Atheist. The witnesses you have to summons are Deacon
Whiffle, Lieut. *Nathaniel Scant, John Fox,* Mrs. *Prim,* Capt. *Timon,* and
Paul Shephard. Bless my body, I'd forgot that *Phoebus,* who is also called
Apollo, was then passing from *Pisces* to *Aquarius;* both Dr. *Pip* and myself
will be as good witnesses as you can get; add our names.

CHUCKLE. Let your *strology* say what it will, I don't like two of the
witnesses, viz. Capt. *Timon* and *Shephard,* for *Timon* is accounted an honest
man, and will speak the truth, and I dare warrant *Atticus* will object against
Shephard, for he was lately convicted for stealing, and for taking a false oath
too; and if he is recorded for perjury, he won't be suffered to swear again.

FROTH. Never fear that, he an't recorded; though he came pretty near to
it; but then it was before another justice, who strained the matter very high.
As to his theft, he has repented and made his peace with the Church, and if
Atticus should object, Deacon *Whiffle* (which by the bye is the reason I'd
have him summoned) will be ready to swear to the sincerity of his repent-
ence.

CHUCKLE. O! if he is *come out**, and is a *New Light*†, he will by no
means answer our purpose.

FROTH. There you are mistaken again, he will have greater liberty and
freedom of mind to speak than he had before. I see this proved the other day,
in a book of *hymns,* entitled *Hudibras,* written by the pious and reverend Mr.
Butler of Old England. I will repeat you the passage that convinced me.

> For saints may do the same things by
> The spirit, in sincerity;
> Which other men are tempted to,
> And at the Devil's instance do:
> For as on land there is no beast,
> But in some fish at sea's exprest;
> So in the wicked there's no vice,
> Of which the saints have not a spice;
> And yet the thing, that's pious in
> The one, in t'other is a sin.[2]

* A common cant expression for a *New Light.*
† A member of a group in sympathy with religious revivalism in 18th century America, i.e., followers of Jonathan Edwards, Campbellites, etc. (ed.)

CHUCKLE. I don't understand verses much, but I heard the Deacon say something like it the other day: I'll e'en do as you advise.

FROTH. So do; you're heartily welcome to all I can advise you to. However, if you by my help, recover what I find you will, (if I have not miscalculated) you will be richly able to afford your witnesses 20 £ a piece.

CHUCKLE. How much shall I get?

FROTH. Not less than a thousand pounds. As to what you said about *Timon,* he is an honest man, and so accounted; and if we can get him of our side, so much the better: *Atticus,* to my knowledge, once highly affronted him, and it is well known that he can't forget nor forgive any that he imagines has done him an injury; I think he'll answer the end very well. You'd better hasten back to the *Justice;* we have been longer in conversation than I intended; the sun was but just arrived at the *Dragon's head* when you came, and now it is almost got to his *tail;* I've a patient I must visit before it is quite passed by, or he cannot survive six hours; so your humble servant.

CHUCKLE. Farewell. [*Exit Chuckle and Froth*]

Justice's house. Enter Chuckle.

CHUCKLE. Well, *Curnal,* I've got back again.

JUSTICE. So I see; pray where have you been all this time? I would not have met with such a chagrin for fifty guineas: Mr. Justice *Riggle* and Mr. Councellor *Trim* did me the honour of a visit, intending to have dined here to-day; but I was so immersed in your affair, that I had only just time to pay them the usual compliment: They have taken their tour to Mr. Secretary *Skinner's,* there to dine; my dinner's all cold! Have you anything more to say? Here's the warrant.

CHUCKLE. I want a number of witnesses summoned.

JUSTICE. I cannot stay to write a *subpoena,* I will put them at the bottom of the warrant: What are their names?

CHUCKLE. Deacon *Whiffle.*

JUSTICE. Well—

CHUCKLE. Lieut. *Nathaniel Scant.*

JUSTICE. A good man.

CHUCKLE. *John Fox.*

JUSTICE. Right.

CHUCKLE. Mrs. *Prim.*

JUSTICE. Ah!

CHUCKLE. Capt. *Timon.*

JUSTICE. I guess that's a mistake!

CHUCKLE. *Paul Shephard.*

JUSTICE. Well thought on.

CHUCKLE. *William Froth* and Dr. *Pip*.

JUSTICE. Better still; carry this to an officer, and don't fail of being here to-morrow morning, at nine o'clock; I must not expect any variation, as to the time.

CHUCKLE. Farewell. [*Exit Chuckle*]

JUSTICE. Servant, you must rise early in the morning, and set my office in order, and acquaint Mrs. *Beau* that I must breakfast at half after seven, precisely: Be sure to see my wig is combed and well powdered; that *Cato* brings my new shoes from Mr. *Squirt*'s shop.

SERVANT. Yes, Sir.

JUSTICE. You impudence, who bid you speak before I had done; see the long table is brought in, and set as far as the house will permit, from my great chair; and that it stands in its proper place; order Mr. *Snipper,* my taylor, to see it covered with black tammy. I shall go into my office at fifty minutes after eight; and do you stand at the gate, and let me know the moment you see them coming, that I may have time to seat myself.

SERVANT. I will be punctual, Sir.

[*Exit Justice and Servant*]

Officer's house. Enter Chuckle.

CHUCKLE. Officer, here is a warrant for you to apprehend one *Atticus,* and summons the within named witnesses.

OFFICER. I shall obey the warrant.

[*Exit Officer and Chuckle*]

Justice's Office. Enter Justice and Servant.

SERVANT. They are coming, Sir.

JUSTICE. When they arrive, introduce the officer to me.

[*Enter Officer, Atticus, &c.*]

OFFICER. Sir, here is the prisoner.

JUSTICE. Place the criminal properly: Your warrant, Mr. Officer.—Silence! —ATTICUS, you are now to attend to a complaint, made on oath before me, by *Ezekiel Chuckle,* and *Sarah* his wife, that you, the said *Atticus,* did, some time between the middle of July, and the last of August, 1768, by force and arms, commit a *Rape* on the body of the said *Sarah,* and divers other enormities, then and there did; all which are against the peace of our Lord the King, &c.

"——ss.

To the sheriff or marshall of our county, or either of their Deputies, Greeting.

"IN his Majesty's name, you are hereby required to take the body of *Atticus,* and him safely keep, that he may be had before me, Colonel *Josiah Beau,* Esq; Justice of peace, and of the quorum, that he may be dealt with, as to the matter of the above complaint, as I shall think proper. Hereof, &c.

"——ss.

"I have brought the within named *Atticus,* and summoned the witnesses. — — *Dep. Sher."*

Atticus, what say you to this charge, are you guilty, or not guilty?

ATTICUS. Not guilty.

JUSTICE. You might, I think, use a little more manners, *not guilty, Sir,* would have been full as becoming for a man in your circumstances; but *Atticus,* to shew you my lenity, and that I have no desire to expose you to shame, reproach and punishment, before I enter on this trial, I freely give you liberty to satisfy, in private the complainants.

LAWYER RATTLE. As the plaintiff's counsel, I second your honour's motion: If *Atticus* will satisfy my client, (and if he has not money sufficient by him, we will take his security,) and ask forgiveness of your honour, at the same time he returns you his thanks, which he ought to do on his knees, I am freely willing not to enter any further on the examination, but bury the matter in oblivion: What say, *Atticus?*

ATTICUS. I shall not comply.

JUSTICE. I shall then proceed to trial; are the witnesses all present?

OFFICER. All but Mr. *William Froth* and *Paul Shephard.*

JUSTICE. What is the reason they did not attend at the time.

DOCTOR PIP. I can plead excuse for Mr. *Froth:* I was obliged myself to visit sundry patients this morning, and sent him to several others under my care, particularly to Mrs. *Whiffle;* her case is very singular and dangerous, she had a *caries* in the second of the *dentes molares,* in the inferior *maxilaris;* as she was eating cherries, she unfortunately broke the *caries* bone with a cherry stone, and largely fractured the *maxilaris,* which has been followed with a train of direful symptoms.

JUSTICE. Do you imagine, Sir, it is hastening to *amputation!*

DOCTOR. I shall use all my endeavours to preserve it for the sake of her *mastication.*

JUSTICE. I excuse Mr. *Froth:* Can anyone answer for *Shephard?*

OFFICER. None, Sir.

JUSTICE. I will swear those that are here: Hold up your hands; you solemnly swear, &c.—Mrs. *Chuckle,* you are the first that must give us your evidence, and dear Ma'am, for God's sake, recollect every circumstance.

Mrs. CHUCKLE. What I have to say is what I said before, only I forgot to tell you, he *kist* me twice, pulled off his hat and drank some water. I need not repeat all I said before, need I?

JUSTICE. No, Ma'am, I'll read the court a copy of your first evidence. [*Justice reads, 'Atticus came, &c.'*]

Mrs. CHUCKLE. There is one thing more, Sir, which I mistook in, when I swore before; I remember now very well, that I told my husband of it as soon as he came home;—that's all.

JUSTICE. Very well, make a minute of what she has added, Mr. *Rattle*.

LAWYER RATTLE. I have, Sir; it was very material.

JUSTICE. Well, *Atticus,* you have heard her complaint read, and also what she has now added: If you have any questions to ask her, you now have liberty.

LAWYER. *Atticus,* his honour is extremely humane.

ATTICUS. [*To Mrs. Chuckle*] Did ever I offer you any affront at the time you guess at, or was you really offended with me.

Mrs. CHUCKLE. I don't remember I was, but I have been mad since.

RATTLE. The criminal's question is impertinent; it is impossible that Mrs. *Chuckle,* or any body else, can remember a bare passion of the mind, two long years.

JUSTICE. You are very right, Sir. Mr. *Chuckle,* favour the court with your evidence.

MR. CHUCKLE. All my wife says is true; she told me *on't* as soon as I came home that night. *Caesar,* one of our neighbour's negro's, said she told him of it next morning.

Mrs. CHUCKLE. So I did.

JUSTICE. *Caesar* should have been here. Officer, he is in the other room, bring him in.

[*Officer exit, and re-enters with Caesar*]

JUSTICE. Well, *Caesar,* did Mrs. *Chuckle* ever tell you any thing about *Atticus's* abusing her.

CAESAR. Yesa, Maser, *he* tell me that *Atticus* he went to bus 'em one day, and a shilde cry, and so he let 'em alone.

JUSTICE. How came she to tell you of this.

CAESAR. Cause, Maser, I bus *him* myself.

JUSTICE. You black impudent villain, begone!

LAWYER. May it please your honour, the negro's evidence makes nothing for, or against the criminal, because it is not allowed by law, for a negro to swear against any white man.

JUSTICE. If I had considered that, I should not have sent for him. Deacon *Whiffle,* you are the first evidence; what have you to say against the prisoner?

DEACON. Nothing; please your honour, Sir, I don't know anything about it; cha, cha, only I've heard he is an Arminian, and don't believe original sin, and all that, which, please your honour, Sir, we read in the bible; I don't know any thing else, cha, cha, please your honour, Sir.

JUSTICE. You may set down, *Deacon.* Lieut. *Nathaniel Scant,* give us your evidence.

LIEUT. SCANT. May it please your honour, I cannot swear that I saw the fact committed, but then I believe it as much as if I had; for I was the first person that told Mr. *Chuckle* his danger, if he did not prosecute, and offered him all the assistance that lay in my power to afford him; for I think it a great pity that all such villains, should not be brought to condign punishment. Mr. *Chuckle* at first, seem'd very unwilling to prosecute, but I used such reasons, as made him resolve otherwise. I said *I none* doubted your honour would assist him as much as possible, consistent with your honour's character: I added, I had often been the means of bringing the guilty to punishment, even where a length of time had made them secure; and instanced in an old fellow, that deserted out of the army in Queen Anne's war, and had escaped 'till the year 1762; your honour remembers I brought him before you, and received the bounty.

JUSTICE. Right, Sir.

LIEUT. SCANT. But as for *Atticus,* I am glad with my whole soul, that he's like to be put out of the way: I have suffered more by him than all the people in town beside, for he has so artfully and wickedly belied me, that he has greatly hurt my custom; he first said my measures were not large enough, which, though utterly false, I was obliged to alter, (your honour knows I suppose that I am an innholder) then he had the impudence in company, of twitting me of selling water instead of rum, and it was impossible for me to prove otherwise, for a single drop casually dropt in, would have made the oath too ensnaring, for any of my customers to take, or otherwise I should have pursued him in law: Another abuse I shall tell your honour, would exceed your belief, was I not under a solemn oath; he called at my house one evening, and called for a pint of cherry, he tasted it, spit it out, and said it was flat; you ought, says he, to be presented, for cheating people as you do; immediately he arose and left the house, neither drinking nor paying for what he called for; the company followed: that single night was ten shillings damage to me; then he procured somebody to make verses about me.

LAWYER. Were you pointed out plainly in them?

SCANT. Yes, Sir.

LAWYER. Was his name to them?

SCANT. No, Sir, but he learn't them to some boys first, and they sang them in my hearing.

LAWYER. This, may it please your honour, is libelling in the strictest sense.

JUSTICE. I take it so, but we should be better informed as to the nature of the offence, if the ballad was produced.

SCANT. I've a copy of it in my pocket.

JUSTICE. Mr. *Lawyer,* be so good as to read it.

[Lawyer reads]

"How can you so basely mix cyder with wine?
Add port to your claret, and still genuine:
Adulterate cherry, there's nothing so good,
So of the rest of your spirits you'd be understood
That *aqua communis* is the grandest corrector,
Which you always make use of, unless a detector
Complains of your liquor; O! then you can alter,
So a thief will not steal if sure of the halter,
Ne'er think what we tell you is matter of laughter
Thou'lt be curs'd for't in this world, and damn'd for't hereafter."

JUSTICE. This is highly provoking, but if I may venture to guess, (although I am no critic in law) that the author of those verses, using the word *We,* in the last line but one, will bar any action against him; for by speaking in the plural, it makes the persons that sing or repeat them, become as it were the real authors.

LAWYER. Your honour might have spared your apology; your criticism is extremely just. Mr. *Scant,* I am sorry to tell you that no action can lay against the criminal for this; proceed, Sir.

SCANT. I've nothing more to add as a witness, but I beg his honour's patience, while I vindicate my character before this honourable court.

JUSTICE. This is alien to our business, yet as long as you have suffered by means of the prisoner, I shall grant your request.

SCANT. As to the reflection he has made on my cherry, I will produce your honour the receipt I make it by, which I am ready to swear I never once altered; it is this:—"Take two gallons of *New-England* rum; molasses two quarts; one pint of cherries; of clear spring water, three gallons; mix them well together, and evaporate the water over a gentle fire, then strain off and bottle for use." This excellent cordial spirit, though expensive in the preparation, I have always sold but one shilling in a quart dearer than common cherry rum is sold in the country; and as to what he has said about claret and port wine, it is all over a *libel,* for I never had a drop of any sort of wine in my house, in all my life.

JUSTICE. You are handsomely cleared. But to the present business: Mr. *Fox,* you are the next evidence.

Fox. I am a very old man, almost eighty-five years old; have walked ten miles on foot to-day, by reason of which I am extremely fatigued; if I might have a little longer time to get breath, it would oblige me.

JUSTICE. Mrs. *Prim* is the next: I have not the happiness to know this lady.

MRS. PRIM. I am she: You know Mr. *Prim,* don't you?

JUSTICE. I can't say I do.

MRS. PRIM. I most wonder at that; Mr. *Prim* is a *power* about among great folks, beside, you made Mr. *Prim* a Cor—.

JUSTICE. I did; it has slipt my mind: How many years since is it?

MRS. PRIM. I don't remember neither, exactly; but it was the same year you made every body officers *a'most* in our town.

JUSTICE. It is amazing I cannot recollect!

MRS. PRIM. Oh! I can tell now, it was that year you *gin* the corn to the poor widows, and *that* money to mend the roads; but Esquire *T—r* went deputy for all.

JUSTICE. The contemptuous treatment I received from the town is fresh in my mind; but Mr. *Prim* still eludes my most careful retrospection.

MRS. PRIM. Why I know that Mr. *Prim* knows you, for I heard Lieut. *Scant* and Mr. *Prim* a talking t'other night, that Mr. *Prim* was to be captain. I believe your honour knows my father-in-law, that is mother's husband.

JUSTICE. Indeed, Ma'am, I am not so happy.

MRS. PRIM. What! don't you know Deacon *Grissel?* I guess you was never up at our meeting: Father always sits in the pulpit, along with the minister, 'cause when father had done being deacon he could not hear.

JUSTICE. We wait your evidence, Ma'am.

MRS. PRIM. I don't love to tell afore so many folks; he is *a nation* bawdy creature to talk, I know. My husband,—

JUSTICE. How did you say, Ma'am?

MRS. PRIM. Mr. *Prim* bought me last week a new water'd silk tabby, to make me a gown *on,* I shewed it to him, and asked him how he liked it? he shook his head and said it look'd as though it was p— p—ist on. Another time he was at our house a *Sabbaday* night, I asked him what made him go out in sermon time; he answered right off, he was so griped in his guts he thought he should have—have—have—*nastied* his breeches, afore he got down stairs; he did not say *nasty,* Sir, he said another word; then we was eating some bread and cheese, and I could not eat another mouthful: That was when we raised our new house, he came swelling up, and told me the punch was not sweet enough; I told him to put his hand in my pocket, and take some loaf sugar, I kept it there 'cause the folks might not get it; then he put his hand in my pocket, but he did not feel for the sugar, Sir: Lud! you can't think how I blush'd. Another time he asked me why widows were easier courted than girls? law! says I, I don't know what is the reason! 'cause, says he, they *know how* better, and a *power* of such talk; besides, folks talk *nationly* about him lately. He went to a house about a fortnight ago, where there was no soul at home but the woman, and staid with her half an hour, all alone.

LAWYER.   Are you positive of this, Ma'am?

MRS. PRIM.   Oh, law! yes, I heard *on't* last *Sabbaday* noon ten times.

JUSTICE.   Has the woman a bad character?

MRS. PRIM.   Why not very bad, Sir, though she will have soon. It wanted *a'most* a fortnight of nine months, when she had her first child, after she was married.

JUSTICE.   How do you know this?

MRS. PRIM.   'Cause, Sir, mother was there herself, and she told me so; more than all that, a great many years ago, he was with some young folks a playing *forfeits,* and he judged some body (he was judge then) to go and kiss one of the young women, and put his hand in her bosom, and keep it there whilst another could count ten; and the girl was forced to let him do that, 'cause that's the play.

JUSTICE.   Do you know this to be true?

MRS. PRIM.   Yes, Sir, as well as I know I am alive.

JUSTICE.   Did you see it yourself?

MRS. PRIM.   No, Sir, but brother *Sam's* wife told me that Cousin *Eunice* see Miss *Sally Faddle,* and her own sister was there, and told her of it. I could tell a thousand such things, I suppose, if I tried, but I won't now; so that's all.

JUSTICE.   You may take your seat, Ma'am. Dr. *Pip,* you are next in turn.

DR. PIP.   Your honour has overlook'd Capt. *Timon.*

JUSTICE.   I have so: I am obliged to you, Sir. Capt. *Timon,* what have you to say?

TIMON.   Some few days before Mr. *Chuckle* commenced this prosecution against *Atticus,* he came to me in a great perplexity, as he said—

LAWYER.   We did not come to hear perplexities. What do you know of the case depending?

TIMON.   By his honour's leave I'll tell you.

JUSTICE. Granted.

TIMON. *Chuckle* desired my advice on what I asked. I have got into the *limbo's,* answered he, my wife in company some time ago, where they were laughing and making themselves merry, hinted or said something against *Atticus's* honour; that *Atticus* was directly informed of it, and intended to prosecute in the severest manner; added further, he was informed that his wife's inadvertency would utterly undo him: I really pitied the man, asked him if there was any foundation for the story? He answered he could not tell, had heard it whispered about several days before his wife told him of it: I then accompanied him to see his wife; she seemed much surprized at my first mentioning of it to her, and said she wished her tongue had been cut out, before she had ever mentioned such nonsense; and had it not been for some neighbour, I should have never thought on't, says she; but on being told they were like to suffer, she had remembered all she could: I asked why she had not complained to her husband, as soon as he came home, if she had been abused; she did not think it worth her while she said: I asked how she ever came to mention it? she answered, that one Widow *Faddle,* (mother to the fore-mentioned Miss *Sally*) came to see her one day, and was full of her stories about this man and t'other, and then like a fool, I said what I did. I then advised Mr. *Chuckle* to compromise the matter with *Atticus,* if possible; but I am heartily surprized to hear Mr. *Chuckle* and his wife both say, that she complained as soon as he came home, when of their own accord, they had told me as before-mentioned.

MRS. CHUCKLE. Why, my husband told me the Lawyer said we ought to have said so at first, to make good—

JUSTICE. Silence! You have no right to dispute with one another; what you have to say, speak to the court. Capt. *Timon,* if you have done I'll proceed to the next examination? Dr. *Pip,* please to favour the court with your evidence.

DR. PIP. May it please your honour, all that I know in the case depending, is, that when Mrs. *Chuckle* was in labour with her last child, I put the question to her in the time of her distress, and she confirmed the truth of what she has now said. She was not frighted, her case was comfortable, and she spoke maturely: As my business is very extensive, I have heard many people speak to his disadvantage: He is certainly of a malevolent detracting constitution. When I performed that famous cure on the person bit with a mad dog, he used his utmost endeavours to make people think my patient was not *hydrophobus,* because he could drink freely.

JUSTICE. The bite of such a mad animal is novel here; the court, Sir, will wait with patience to hear a short description of it.

DOCTOR. I am proud to oblige you, Sir. In the morning of the first of last July, my patient received a wound in his right leg, on the *fibula,* three inches and nine lines below the *pattella,* and two inches and one line from the *crural artery;* the *laceration* was so small as hardly to be seen, but on close inspection, 'twas evident there was a solution of continuity; yet such was the activity of the *canine virus,* that he was seized with all the symptoms of the *rabies,* in its last state, in five minutes after he was bit, and lay perfectly insensible, without action or motion; in this deplorable case I immediately put him into a salivation, which by a method I have of my own, I effected in two hours; as he was, he swallowed large draughts of a *jullep* of my own invention; also which, as it had a kind effect, he kept it by his bed side, and drank at pleasure: This directly took off the *hydrophobia,* and the salivial discharge carried off the *canine spiculæ,* and in forty-eight hours he perfectly recovered. This, Sir, is a true state of the case; yet *Atticus* has had the ill-nature and impudence, to make people believe that my patient was only frighted at a dog barking, and so fell into fits, which it seems he had been used to at other times, but they were not occasioned by the bite of a mad dog, which was the case here; yet he made use of this circumstance to depreciate my character, and tarnish the extraordinary cure I had wrought.

JUSTICE. Your account, Doctor, is as highly satisfactory as the prisoner's base insinuation is abusive; but proceed, Sir.

DOCTOR. I have nothing more to add, only he once had of me a box of *unguentum neapolitanum,* and refused to tell me what he was going to do with it.

JUSTICE. As I do not understand physick, so I know not the nature of the medicine you have mentioned.

DOCTOR. It is, may it please your honour, a mercurial ointment used to destroy a certain pernicious vermin, that are generally found near the posteriors, and also in curing the *lues venerea.*

JUSTICE. And this you are positive he had of you.

DOCTOR. I remember exactly the quantity, six grains,—and further, I have nothing to say.

OFFICER. Mr. *Froth* is just arrived. [*Enter Froth*]

JUSTICE. The court waits Mr. *Froth* for your evidence in the case now pending.

DOCTOR. I beg your honour's pardon to indulge my enquiring first, concerning Mrs. *Whiffle.*

JUSTICE. Granted.

DOCTOR. How did you find her?

FROTH. Her rest last night was somewhat better: she drank while I was there, half a pint of plumb gruel; she had a costly stool the last twenty-four hours, and urined twice, the *maxillum* begins to be exfolded on one side, but there is dangerous flesh on the other side.

DOCTOR. Is the *fungus* spongy or *fistula?*

FROTH. I am apt to think it will get to be a real *fistular* in *ano.*

DOCTOR. I shall hasten to her relief as soon as his honour will permit.

JUSTICE. Proceed, Mr. *Froth.*

FROTH. I have been so extremely busied to-day that I came from home and forgot my calculation, of consequence I cannot be so particular: It is true, may it please your honour, that I cannot swear I saw the fact committed with my own eyes, at the time it was done; but if I may be allowed to swear by the planets, which is as certain, I can swear to the truth of all that has been said by Mrs. *Chuckle,* and the evidences.

JUSTICE. I do not think we are allowed by law, to admit such an evidence, besides if it were allowable, I cannot think you could be so certain from figures, as from ocular demonstration.

FROTH. Every atom, for ocular demonstration is no more than the figure of objects imprinted on the mind: I am sorry I left my books at home, but to let you know that I don't over-rate my knowledge in these nice points, I can tell your honour that before ever Mr. *Chuckle* came to me, I had discovered the whole affair, and had minuted the names of all the witnesses, necessary for him to summons, in my Legerdemain.—'Twas I that many years ago informed Lieut. *Scant,* where he might find an old deserter; I remember I discovered that by observing what an *angle Mars* made with the *Zodiack.* 'Twas I that first discovered that Miss *Peggy Squat* was pregnant, and by whom; this is not by any physical discernment, but by carefully eyeing the twinkling of *Venus* and *Jupiter,* and calculating their distances, mutual attraction and cohesion. 'Twas I that long ago foretold that some of the greatest scoundrels in the country, would rise higher both in dignity and villainy, than your honour. 'Twas I that first—

JUSTICE. Not quite so fast, Sir. I desire to be satisfied as to the last mentioned fact, for if that be true I shall believe all you say.

LAWYER. Your honour will have good right to; but Mr. *Froth* made a little slip in language, in coupling dignity and villainy as he did.

DOCTOR. I beg pardon for Mr. *Froth;* he never has had the advantage of an academical education as your honour, Mr. *Rattle,* and I have.

FROTH. May it please your honour, I only meant that villains that was once below your honour, are now above you.

JUSTICE. I am not nice about words; I want to be fully satisfied as to the facts.

FROTH. Please to ask Mr. *Shephard* on this point.

JUSTICE. What do you know *Shephard*, of what Mr. *Froth* has now said?

SHEPHARD. Mr. *Froth* told me that he knew when Mr. *W-s-l-e* and yourself, was in commission of the peace together, you would never rise higher than to be a colonel, and the other to be the first man in the p—c—.

JUSTICE. Mr. *Froth,* I am fully convinced: How came you to know this?

FROTH. It was, Sir, by casting a figure; as the scheme is mislaid, it has slipt my memory; I will recollect it some future time.

JUSTICE. I should take it as a great favour.

FROTH. If I may resume what I was saying before, I was the first that dif—

JUSTICE. Good Sir, spare yourself the trouble, I am fully convinced as to your skill in this noble science.

LAWYER. I am fully of your honour's mind. Mr. *Froth's* skill is unquestionable. I can't say that I see any further need of evidence; yet Mr. *Shephard* and Mr. *Fox* are to be examined; but *Atticus* you had better plead guilty and save the court trouble.

JUSTICE. You see he stands hardened. Mr. *Shephard,* relate to the court what you know concerning the facts charged on the criminal.

SHEPHARD. As I was passing by the house of—

ATTICUS. With your honour's leave I object against this witness.

JUSTICE. If you have the least colour of reason for your objection, he shall be debarred.

ATTICUS. I think I have reason sufficient; he has been proved and recorded guilty of theft and lying, and it were also very easy to convict him of perjury.

JUSTICE. If this be true, (though I doubt it) you have good grounds for your objection. Are there any present that can speak to this?

FROTH. Sir, I knew at first that the prisoner would make this objection against *Shephard,* but he has long since repented, and is now a worthy man. Will your honour ask Deacon *Whiffle?*

JUSTICE. It will give me more satisfaction to hear what *Shephard* has to say for himself.

SHEPHARD. I cannot deny what has been said by the poor prisoner; but I will tell your honour that about four years ago I was under conviction, and saving conversion;* yet after this I fell away, and was so tempted by the Devil, who made me believe that if I was under a necessity, I had a right to

---

* By exhibiting these characters of hypocrisy, nonsense, slander and deceit, (which are taken from the real life) the compiler means no reflection on religion, or any of the sincere professors of it, of what denomination soever.

take what I pleased, so I took from several neighbours a few sheep; it was not more than thirty or forty, and was left to charge it on an innocent man, and was also nearly left to swear to it, but I was happily prevented and brought to see the evil of what I had done, and I think I had a more clear discovery than I had heretofore; but I was in great distress before I received satisfaction, and applied myself to Deacon *Whiffle,* who I must say was a very great help to me.

JUSTICE. By a plain law your evidence cannot be admitted.

LAWYER. It is true there is a sham law of the province against such evidence, but by ecclesiastick law he has a right to swear, if he has made peace with the religious society of which he was a member.

JUSTICE. I am obliged to you, Sir, for this information. If he is a member of your society, Deacon, please to inform us.

DEACON. May it please your honour, Sir, he is a brother, and as himself has just said, was some years ago savingly wrought on, but through the temptation of the wicked adversary of precious souls, he fell away, but after he was convicted he came through great goodness to a wonderful sight of his sins, and was in great horror until he came and confessed them to me, and I was enabled through mercy to afford him comfort, cha, cha, I told him, may it please your honour, Sir, that near thirty-five years ago I passed a change, which I desire to be thankful I shall never forget, but after this I was left to great buffetings of Satan, and I was enabled to tell him how wonderfully I had been dealt with and delivered; I passed many years I may say almost without a wicked thought or action: From thence I was lifted up with spiritual pride, then Satan was let loose upon me, he appeared at first as an angel of light: I very well remember the first time I discovered him was, as I was running a line of division with one of my neighbours, in the form of a stake and heap of stones, which he made me confident was the real bound, 'till the surveyor convinced me that it was a mistake, and then I was enabled to see that the stake and heap of stones, was none other than the Devil tempting me to wrong my neighbour; and this passage was set home on my mind, *Cursed be he that removeth his neighbour's land-mark,* and he immediately disappeared:—After this I passed many years in great consolation, and thought my mountain stood so strong, that it could never be moved; at this time Satan appeared again, in a manner subtle as himself, which betrayed me into both wicked thoughts and actions, for on going into my mill I had a new toll-dish and strike presented me, which I was left to use, and this should never have seen the evil of, had he not gone further in his temptations with me; my half-bushel was lost, and a new one *curiously* made and left in its room, and this I was left to use in a way of trade, till it was challenged; then I plainly saw that toll-dish, strike, and half-bushel was the old serpent, in those various forms that deceived me before, and I escaped as a bird from the fowler's snare. After this I had great peace of conscience for many years together, and lived so exemplary, that I was thought fit to be chosen into the office I am now enabled to sustain, but I had no sooner gone up to the house of the Lord, and opened the psalm-book to find the stanzas, our minister had ordered to be sung, to my amazement, saw a man standing before me, with his hair frizzled, and hanging loose in his neck, his hands and eyes uplifted to heaven, nay every muscle and feature in his face seemed to be as it were so many prayers; this so fixed my attention that I knew nothing that passed, till our minister thumped so loud on the pulpit, that it aroused me, and I immediately recollected it was my old tempter, and that passage came to my mind, *Satan, why troublest thou my servant;* he at once disappeared, since which I have had no more conflicts with him: This so comforted and strengthened dear brother *Shephard,* that in little time his grief abated, he had lively actings. Our church received him as a welcome guest to her bosom; at present he walks worthy of his vocation. And may it please your honour, Sir, don't take it amiss if I tell your honour, Sir, cha, cha, I should believe dear brother *Shephard* as soon as your honour, Sir, or—my —self—Sir.

JUSTICE. Although I must tell you, *Atticus,* your objections cannot be heard, I find by eccesiastick law, which I suppose is founded on that passage, that if your brother trespass against you seventy times seven in a day, and turn again and repent, you are bound to forgive and restore him both as a brother and witness: You are to know that the laws of God are greater than the laws of men. Agreeable then to the old latin maxim, *quod potest majus potest minus,* he must be admitted as an evidence against you. I have taken this pains to convince you of my impartiality, and that you may be left without excuse. Mr. *Shephard,* give your evidence, but speak with caution.

SHEPHARD. I shall speak nothing but the truth: As I was passing by the house of Mr. *Chuckle,* I heard the screaming of a female voice, I hastily left my team, I ran to her relief, not knowing what the matter was 'till I saw the prisoner in the very act, or rather my opening of the door surprised him, and he fled; with my blood boiling in my veins, I pursued him, but fear lent him wings, and as it was just dark, he soon escaped my sight; whilst I was in quest of him my team was started, and being afraid they would over set my sled, I had not time to go back and see what condition Mrs. *Chuckle* was in, since which I have heard nothing of the matter, concluded it was made up, till I received a summons.

JUSTICE. You mention your sled, pray what time of the year was it?

SHEPHARD. The last of January.

JUSTICE. Are you not mistaken, Mr. *Shephard?* It is impossible.

SHEPHARD. I remember the snow was three feet deep.

JUSTICE. Mrs. *Chuckle,* do you remember seeing this witness at that time?

MRS. CHUCKLE. Some body came in, but I was so frighted I could not tell who it was.

JUSTICE. I do not remember your mentioning that you called for help.

MRS. CHUCKLE. I can't say I did, Sir, but I was in such confusion,—I can't—

LAWYER. When we have gone through the examination, I can easily reconcile this seeming difference.

JUSTICE. I shall wait for your explication. The last evidence is Mr. *Fox.*

Fox. This prisoner is a very subtle, cunning, wicked man. I have taken various methods to entrap him; and as I am an old man, I may without vanity say, that few men in the world are more experienced in plans, intrigues and traps, than I am; yet I never could fully, with all my assiduity, accomplish my design: He has such a number of spies and informers, in every quarter, to watch every motion of them he suspects, that although I have crept after him in the dead hours of the night, and noise itself was as whist as a mouse: When I had almost tracted him to his borough, the barking of a dog, or what is more strange, a coughing at a distance would give him the alarm: Once I thought I had him as safe as an eel in an eel-pot; my son *Joshua's* wife is a bouncing, merry, sly *tike;* as he often frequented the house, I contrived matters with her to out-wit him; she was to be free and familiar, and take all opportunities to jest and scuffle with him; this took place, but unfortunately one day as they were romping together, her apron happened to be misplaced, and her nethermost apparel not being found, he discovered something that was either too forbidding, or he heard me as I was endeavoring to conceal myself under the window, be it which it will, he precipitately left the house, and has never been there since; but my attempts have not been altogether fruitless, for by watching some of his motions, where he was suspected, I have found him out in others equally bad, in which he was not suspected. As I was one day on the scout, I fell in company with one Mr. *Azariah Bluster,* a school-master, who was as inquisitive as myself, in the same affair, but is some times so forward, his designs are too soon and too easily known; he immediately asked my business, I answered I was hunting after some game, and visiting my traps, of which I always keep a good number: Well, said he, I am on another kind of business; that rascally *Atticus,* was justly indebted to me, for which I prosecuted him, but he found means to cheat me of it, and make me pay costs, and now I am out to find some way to make a reprisal on him: Can you prove he cheated you, said I? Without the least doubt, replied he, and was beginning to relate the whole matter, when *Atticus* himself appeared in sight; I desired him to desist, and pursued my game, so that neither *Atticus,* nor Mr. *Bluster* knew my design.

JUSTICE. As the case stands, it is proper to send for Mr. *Bluster;* I determine to have all the light in the affair I can, whether it be for, or against the prisoner, that he may have no reason to complain of partiality.

LAWYER. Your honour has taken infinite pains already; if the criminal had the least feelings of conscience, he would confess, and put an end to this tedious trial.

JUSTICE. Officer, hasten Mr. *Bluster* here as soon as possible. [*Exit Officer*]

Bluster's house. Enter Officer.

OFFICER. Sir, I am sent to inform you that Colonel *Beau,* and Lawyer *Rattle,* desire your immediate attendance.

BLUSTER. I was just beginning one of *Virgil Eclogues,* but I'll gratify their request. [*Exit Officer and Bluster*]

Justice's Office. Enter Officer and Bluster.

OFFICER. The gentleman is come.

JUSTICE. Please, Sir, to let the court hear what you have to offer.

BLUSTER. *Tyterre tu pattala recubas sub fag mane fagi sylvestrem tenui—*

JUSTICE. I must interrupt; you mistake the design of coming here; we want you as an evidence.

BLUSTER. Against whom, my Lord, do you want I should mount the rostrum, and give my deposition *in perpetuam rei memoriam.*

JUSTICE. You mistake my title, Mr. *Bluster,* your Honour, is the common appellation, magistrates are known by in this country.

BLUSTER. I ask pardon of your Honour for mistaking, I had just been reading one of *Marcus Cicero Tully's* orations; indeed I should not have began with a quotation from *Virgil,* had I known for what purpose I was sent for.

JUSTICE. You are quite excusable, Sir: I suppose your coming into this assembly brought to mind some of your juvenile exercises.

BLUSTER. True, may it please your honour, I imagined nothing but that you and Mr. *Rattle* designed to entertain this polite auditory, with a recital of some of my former declamations.

JUSTICE. Indeed, Sir, it was your evidence that is wanted against the prisoner, *Atticus* by name.

BLUSTER. It is on his character, I suppose, Sir.

JUSTICE. Right.

BLUSTER. I have always chose to keep myself free from meddling with other people's characters, and now I most humbly beg your honour would excuse me, for although I know as much of the prisoner as any person alive, I chuse to keep silence.

ATTICUS. By his honour's leave; what mean you, *Bluster,* by this ungenerous insinuation, that you know more than any body else, but choose to keep silence, when it is well known to all that are so unhappy as to be acquainted with you, that you are no small talkative?

BLUSTER. *Pudet hace approbria nobis et diu potuisse, et non potuisse refelli.*

JUSTICE. You should consture your latin.

BLUSTER. As I do not in the least suspect your honour's, the learned Lawyer's and Doctor's accuracy and skill in the classicks, it would be but an ill compliment to translate every *apropos* sentence of the Latin shall make use of; suffice it therefore for the *profanum vulganum* for me to say,

> To bear an open slander, is a curse;
> But not to find an answer, is a worse.

JUSTICE. Then I think for this once you must throw aside your natural modesty, and relate to the court what you know against the prisoner.

BLUSTER. And must I then,—but— *O! Justicia infandum jubes renovare dolorem.* But now, O *Justice!* you command me to repeat horrid woe. This *Atticus,* came to my house at eleven of the clock, A.M. on Wednesday the twenty-fourth of August, *Annoque Domini,* 1767, and there dined with me in the best manner; after dinner he must needs, to divert himself, go into my library, and after having tumbled my books awhile, fell to playing on my English violin, but being ignorant of setting it in tune he broke both my altus and base cords, then impudently laughing, he told me he had broke both my banjor strings for me: This so raised my indignation, to be treated in such an ungentleman-like a manner, that I demanded pay for my violin cords, which he refusing, still insensed me so that I told him in plain English, that if he did not pay me for my fiddle strings, which cost me one shilling and four pence, I would prosecute him for his dinner also. He repeated another sneer of contempt, and abruptly went off. I then issued a prosecution against him for eight shillings and eight pence, before Justice *Wright:* on trial he suborned a false witness, to swear that I invited him to dinner, and he was allowed to swear that he broke my violin cords by accident; so the Justice gave the case against me with the costs, but I am bold to say the prisoner is foresworn.

JUSTICE. You should not be too peremptory, Sir.—Your charge for his dinner appears to me a little exaggerated.

LAWYER. Not only your honour, but an angel cannot judge the justice of the demand, unless they could see the account.

JUSTICE. Right.

BLUSTER. Here is the same account I commenced prosecution on.

JUSTICE. Mr. *Lawyer,* please to read it.

[*Lawyer reads*]
B—e, *August* 24th, 1767.

ATTICUS to Mr. *Azariah Bluster,* A. M.—*Dr.*

	£.			
To misplacing my reading place mark, in the famous history of (a lap dog) Pompey the little.	£.	0	0	2	0
To two violin cords that you broke,		0	1	4	0
To buying new ditto, and tuning them,		0	1	8	0
To dining at my house, – – – –		0	2	0	0
To the use of a china plate for pudding and sauce, – – – –		0	0	9	½
To the use of one silver plate, –		0	0	9	½
To the use of one London pewter ditto,		0	0	4	½
To the use of one silver handled knife and fork, – – – –		0	0	10	0
To two glasses of sweet wine, –		0	0	6	0
To three pipes of tobacco, –		0	0	1	½
To one pipe that you broke, –		0	0	1	0
	£.	0	8	8	0

LAWYER. I think, may it please your honour, Mr. *Bluster's* account is very reasonable; your honour did not consider the extraordinary expense of procuring and fixing new cords to his violin.

JUSTICE. I am fully convinced, Sir, of Mr. *Bluster's* honesty, but you know, Sir, every Justice has his method. There is room, Mr. *Bluster,* for an appeal.

LAWYER. By the date it is out-lawed.

JUSTICE. I am sorry, Sir; Have you any thing further to add?

BLUSTER. *Non domino.*

LAWYER. *May it please your honour,*

YOUR honour hath at length (with more than humane patience) gone through this long, this tedious, this (if I may so call it) black catalogue of evidence, against the criminal, by which we have his character set in a most glaring light, and the fact alledged against him incontestibly proved: But, may it please your honour, because there appears some seeming difference in the relation of the witnesses, which by the bye, is no uncommon thing, where they are so numerous,—I shall,—*First.* Reconcile those seeming disagreements: *Secondly,* Consider his character in general. *Thirdly,* Prove that he designed to commit the fact alledged against him. *Fourthly,* Show that such design renders him really guilty in law, and consequently obnoxious to punishment. But *First,* As to the disagreement of the witnesses. There seems to be some little mistake lie between Mr. *Chuckle,* his wife, and Capt. *Timon,* as to the time she first complained to her husband. As *Timon's* evidence is but one, and both Mr. *Chuckle* and his wife do now remember what at first they had forgot; I think for my part, *Timon's* deposition ought by no means to be credited; but granting *Timon* was in the right, and that they in their great hurry and fright are mistaken, it does not militate against the spirit of the charge. Cannot your honour easily conceive how much she must be disconcerted, from such an attack? That her modesty, triumphed as it were at first over her honour, and would not permit her to relate to her bosom friend, her other self, the indignity she had received. I say modesty, the beauty and guard of female honour, resisted even the violence of passion such abuse had raised; what reluctance must she feel, when to reserve her virtue untarnished, she was obliged to inform that person, who of all others, would hold it most in abhorrence, and whose peace of all others, she most feared to disturb. It is a tender case for a wife,—for a wife I say,—to relate to her husband,—her husband,—such conduct as would excite that jealousy which is the rage of a man. For my part it gives me exquisite pain,—nay, I even sympathize with her in that hour of trial, when she first began the dire relation to her husband. It is not any ways unaccountable then, that she should mistake a little at times: It was always in her mind, and though in reality it was a fortnight,—a month,—or ever two months after, it appeared as the same instant to her: For, may it please your honour, it is the succession of ideas in our mind, that we distinguish time by, and no other idea being in her mind, but of this horrid affair, it must of consequence appear to her the identical point of time the fact was committed; but on the first relation to her husband, other ideas took place, viz. grief, fear of his anger, and the like. I *none* doubt she told her husband he was just fled, for as has been proved, the idea of this assassin was continually in her mind, till she acquainted her husband. This point then, may it please your honour, is as clear as the noon day sun.—To proceed; *Shephard's* evidence will at first sight appear as a flat contradiction to the complainant's oath; but it is very evident that the circumstances of the sled has led Mr. *Shephard* into a mistake, as to the time of the year, but this is easily accounted for, *Shephard's* recollecting his having his sled with him, made him conclude there was snow, and of consequence that it was winter; not considering that sleds are used at other times in the year, as a carriage for heavy articles, so that it may notwithstanding be in the summer, as my clients have sworn: His mentioning her screaming, which it seems she has forgot, is in no degree strange; persons in a fright it is well known, can neither hear or speak at some times. May it please your honour, in a fright, there is such a dissipation of the animal spirits that there is not a sufficient quantity in the auditory nerve, to impress the sensorium with the idea of sound, from the modulated air in the ear, so that she might scream as loud as she could hallo, and never hear herself, from the reason just mentioned: This being so, *Shephard's* deposition stands good, and he, your honour remembered, saw the man in the very fact, or very near it.

JUSTICE.   It could not be in the fact, according to Mrs. *Chuckle's* oath.

LAWYER.   It might, Sir, notwithstanding what she has said, for in a fright the senses are all more or less treacherous, and there might have been a privation of feeling, as well as hearing. However, let that be as it may, he saw enough to corroborate what she has said: I know of no other part or parts of evidence that need any further explanation here. I shall therefore, *Secondly,* consider his character in the general: And may it please your honour, there is not a grain,—not a grain,—no not the smallest atom of evidence, but preponderates the scale on my client's side. The obscenity of his conversation with Mrs. *Prim,* is plainly indicative of the impurity of his intentions; his squalid triteness on her taby, was very unchaste, and still further develops to view the debauchery of his mind, nor less indelicate was the cause of his leaving the house of God, but more especially is to be noted, his haunting the house mentioned by this witness. It is impossible to think of the least excuse for him—I speak it with the greatest moral certainty—when I say,—it must be unlawful for him to consume away thirty minutes with a married woman, alone, who it seems has not the best character neither: This was taken so heinous by some of his godly neighbours, they could not forebear mentioning of it to one another, on the Lord's day. His refusing to answer Dr. *Pip's* interrogatories, is a circumstance by no means in his favour, and must lead us to suppose that the questioned mercurial was not the only one he made use of: It would be superfluous to tell your honour, the *lues venera* submits to no other medicine. Can your honour think any other by Mr. *Fox's* evidence, than that Mr. *Joshua's* wife would have shared the same fate with my client, if the criminal had not been hindered by some unlucky accident. But his character will appear all of a piece, if we consider him as a neighbour; his malevolence to Doctor *Pip* is almost too much for human patience to bear: When the Doctor had with such surprizing skill and expedition, rescued his patient from the jaws of death, and expelled the most violent of all poisons, the *canine virus,* then to insinuate forsooth, it was only a meer fright at the growling of a dog. O! HORRENDUM! Nor can I pass by his ludicrous treatment of generous and benevolent Lieut. *Scant,* without notice; to fall unprovoked on so good and useful a member of society, is no venal crime. If such things are passed over without our showing a due contempt of them, it will serve to discourage all public virtue and merit: To wrong a man of his good name, is equally heinous as to wrong him of his estate, but it seems he values neither name or estate. We have just had the most glaring instance of his knavery to that learned gentleman, I mean Mr. *Bluster.* This gentleman, may it please your honour, has plumply sworn that the prisoner wittingly and willingly cheated him, or in other words, feloniously took from him part of his interest; and though the debt was not large, the crime was equally wicked, for if his opportunity had been larger, there is room to doubt but the same inclination would have increased in proportion. He has further intimated that the prisoner can easily dispense with perjury. Why need I take up time in a case so plain? I shall only add that his morals and doctrines are much alike:—Deacon *Whiffle* does not plainly say he is an Atheist, but calls him an Arminian, which is almost as bad:—Indeed if I—

DEACON GRISSEL. I can't hold in any longer, I must speak to this point myself.

LAWYER. It is contrary to the rules of court to interrupt an attorney.

DEACON. Well be it so, I am an old man, I know more about this matter than you do; I've been a church member fifty-five years, and a deacon one and thirty; come, come, hear what I have to say.

LAWYER. I submit the matter to his honour.

JUSTICE. It will be well, Sir, to hear what the aged gentleman has to say.

DEACON. Why there, Mr. Lawyer, I told you so.—I say right off he is an Atheist, and I really believe he is one, and I have good reason to think so, for when the house of my God was building at *B—t—e,* on which I laid out so much of my temporal estate, he like *Sanballet* and *Tobiah,* in good old *Nehemiah's* time, endeavoured to hinder, or at least did not promote that good work.

ATTICUS. I was expressly forbid by the Deacon, to have any thing to do with it, may it please your honour.

DEACON. In answer to you, Mr. Impudence, I only forbid your having any thing to do with things that were sanctified to an holy use, such as the cushion over which our minister delivers us the oracles of God: I said, and I say again, you had no right to meddle with; for it would be a dreadful profanation of the church's holiness, to receive any part of its sanctified utensils, from an unbeliever. But this did neither hinder nor forbid your joining to help procure the earthly materials, such as the timber, boards, nails, laths, stones, and the like: This is what, honoured Sir, I charge him with, and what I have to say is, that if a man will not lay out his money or goods towards the house of God, when called upon by his spiritual father to do it, he believes nothing in the God of the house, when finished. I don't speak this from any prejudice I have against him, for I never said one word, while my son the Doctor was giving in his evidence for, and though he was greatly abused. But I shan't say no more.

LAWYER. I shall resume what I was saying. The worthy Deacon has been so pertinently intelligible, that comment is needless. Indeed if I am not mistaken, Mr. *Froth* has hinted that he had discovered by the planets, Atheistical principles in him, so that it may be literally said, his impiety and immorality has reached the very heavens, and are visible in the constellation, and doubtless are now crying for vengeance, on his guilty head, which it is to be hoped will soon overtake him. I come *Thirdly,* to prove, he designed to commit the fact alledged. As his general character has been thoroughly scaned, I need say nothing of it here, but would just observe that the least circumstance against him weighs full as much as a positive evidence against an honest man.———May it please your honour, when I take but a single glance of the pregnant proofs of his design, I am struck with astonishment, that the wretched criminal can front it any longer, as he remains hardened in obstinacy; I proceed to say, first—the bare abrupt question—Is your husband at home? is naturally construed to imply he wished he was not, hoping in his absence to gain his point—the innocent (intended) victim answered, No. —What was the next step?—to seat himself in her lap—a modest situation this!—proceeding, he first placed his hand on her bosom,—and next on her knee—can your honour doubt, but that he had the medium in his eye?—It should seem by the evidence, that he arose from this situation—being assured of victory—and asked for water—a plain indication he had long formed the design, and that the urgency of some nameless vessel, had brought on a general inflammation—the next point he gained was the bed—a place he knew well enough not made wholly for sleep—at this arrival he did not forget to salute her—can any thing be more plain than what he was now designing? Your honour remembers what the poet says,

——That a kiss
Is a prelude to the succeeding acts of bliss:

If the rhyme had allowed, the poet would have said lust.—At this critical juncture, a child cried—this with *Shephard's* approach alarmed the letcher and he fled.—May it please your honour, we can nearly in this case, adapt the sacred passage, *the wicked flee when no man pursueth.*—By this time it plainly appears that he premeditately designed to what was alledged against him, and that nothing less than omnipotent interposition preserved the gentlewoman's virtue and innocence, and protected her from ruin.—It now only remains, to shew that he stands really guilty in the eye of the law and consequently obnoxious to the punishment.—It is, may it please your honour, the designs of men that distinguish them from brutes and mere machines, for example, may it please your honour, suppose a man *paralytick* or in a fit of convulsions, should kill his neighbour—could your honour think fit to punish such a man any more than you would a wind-mill that did the same to a man that came within the reach of its arms? Again, if a man in his sleep should commit such an action, that if he were awake it would be fornication, and even issue should follow such embrace, the man (proving himself a-sleep) could not be chargable in law either with fornication or bastardy, a whit more than the wind-mill of murder, because it would be evident he acted not from design—but if we were to suppose (to make the matter still plainer) that such an action was to be committed by a man partly awake and partly asleep, would not such lethargic state in a great measure abate the criminality in your honour's mind—surely—this being granted, then I argue, that if actions absolutely committed, without design, are not punishable, then *vice versa* wicked designs without actions are punishable. I take it, that what distinguishes a man to be awake from one that is asleep, is design, if therefore it is design and that only, that constitutes actions virtuous or vicious; the criminal is in fact guilty.—It may be that some in this case may object and say this, as the fact was not absolutely committed the action is wanting—to this I answer that the design is an action—designs are positions of the mind, when there are no positions in the mind it is perfectly inactive, and is as really a blank as a writ before the clerk has signed it and the Lawyer filled it up.—That positions are actions is evident, further from this, that without positions there could be no muscular motion; the illustrious Van Helmart says, that it is an *archeus,* i. e. spirit or position that resides in and moves every muscle of the body.—It follows therefore from what has been said, that the designs of men are what ought principally to be attended to, and that muscular actions are only the effects, not the cause of design—If this reasoning be just, which I think none will deny, the case stands thus, whoever designs to commit a rape is in fact guilty of the same. But it is proved that the prisoner did design to commit a rape—therefore the prisoner is in fact guilty of commiting a rape.—We wait only for your honour's determination and sentence.

Deacon Grissel. I have stood a long time in astonishment to hear the

Lawyer talk, but held my tongue that he might not twit me of putting him out again. But Sir, he has not said what he ought first to have said, and I dare not in conscience and the fear of the Lord omit it. In the 5 c. of M—— and 28v. are these words recorded, *whosoever looketh on a woman to lust after her hath committeth adultery with her.*[3] Here it is plain that only looking on a woman is committing adultery. The Lawyer I think calls it a rape, but the Bible calls it adultery,—as we are not to be wise above what is written, I shall follow the Bible; he did more than to look: He went as far as feeling, he could not have done but one thing more. Your honour is not to understand that a common looking is meant in the text, but such looking as creates in a man a different feeling than what is natural. This is the committing adultery in the text. I do not doubt the prisoner has committed adultery ten times in a spiritual sense since he has been in this house. Indeed it is not such a difficult matter to do as most people imagine, the difficulty lies in not doing it. That is not so uncommon as may be imagined. I will tell you what happened in my parish some years ago: Our last minister had been a painful labourer in the vineyard among us, in word and doctrine for many years, at last he looked on a woman to lust after her, and she told of it. I immediately summoned the church together, who all severally questioned him if he had any unlawful doings with her, which he denied. I then solemnly put the question to him myself, in these words, Mr. E-l-n, do not you think, that if restraining grace had not hindered, you should have done wickedly with her. The poor man with tears in his eyes answered he did not know but he should. We thereupon dismissed him immediately from the pastoral office among us: Thus you see, Sir, that ministers as well as wicked men are sometimes tardy in this point, though it is not always found out, but when it is I think it ought always to be punished — — — you are wise enough I hope to take the hint.

JUSTICE. If no body present has any thing further to offer I shall proceed to sentence. Officer, first clear the court of all but Mr. *Rattle* and myself, that we may have time to make up judgment in form.—Servant, fill me a glass of Maderia—I feel faint. [*Exit all but Justice and Lawyer*] Mr. Lawyer, I want your opinion in private on this affair, for notwithstanding you have argued masterly and logically in this case: Nay, I think I may say without compliment that you have even surpassed yourself in eloquence and strength of argument: Yet we see it has not the desired effect, but he stands out and refuses either to acknowledge or compound, and now not having the proof we hoped to have, how shall we contrive matters to save ourselves and not lose our cost and trouble.

LAWYER. I cannot find words to express my sensibility of the honour you do me: I shall readily give you my advice on this head. It is well, Sir, we are in private, for the prisoner nor the rabble have any right to know the motives you act from in this case. Will your honour believe me when I say that I laboured the point much longer than I should, hoping it would terrify the villain to a compliance, that your honour might have an ample reward for your pains, for your honour well knows, that whether he was proved guilty or not guilty, I was sure of my own fee from the plaintiff.

JUSTICE. Your complaisance, Sir, fills me with too an agreeable pleasure for utterance, and the only way that ever I can make you amends will be to recommend all distressed and injured persons to your advice and patronage. —You cannot think, Sir, it would be adviseable to inflict on him any corporal punishment?

LAWYER. By no means; but then I would mulct him to the King, which comes to you as his representative.

JUSTICE. If he should appeal, will it not appear we had no right to fine him?

LAWYER. It may if the matter is strictly examined, but then you well know that if he should appeal, his tryal must come on before Justice *Gripe* and old Justice *Poppy,* who are seldom known to alter judgment in these cases.

JUSTICE. Granted, but then the fine will fall out of our hands.

LAWYER. True, Sir.

JUSTICE. Had not I better then give him such an admonition as will tend to soften him, at the same time let him know that it is my clemency that dismisses him with only taking costs?

LAWYER. I ingeniously believe your honour has hit on the best expedient.

JUSTICE. Will you please to make out the bill in form. Sir, the Sum total is   £. 1 16 0.

[Lawyer writes and afterwards reads]

—ss.

"*AT a trial held before* Josiah Beau, *Esq;* &c."

"To warrant, trial, judgment, Lawyer's fee, &c. &c.

£. 16 1 0

According to your desire, here it is, Sir.

JUSTICE. You have made a great mistake, Sir.

LAWYER. As how, Sir.

JUSTICE. Please to recollect your figures.

LAWYER. Bless my body, so I have; I beg pardon, Sir: The natural obliquity of my eyes inverted the figures—you are quite right, Sir,—it is—surely enough.

[Alters the figures] £. 1 16 0

JUSTICE. It is right now, Sir. Order the Officer in with the prisoner.—
[Enter Officer, prisoner, &c]

SILENCE! —————— IT was the saying—of a wise man—(worth
to be written—in capitals of gold)—that a coward—has fought—that a coward has conquered—but a coward never forgave—it is only great—minds that
are capable of this virtue.—I—have no room to doubt but—that this audience
will be greatly surprised at my sentence in this case—and you *Atticus* in
particular—(from the guilt of your own conscience) have no reason to expect
any other than the severest doom.—But—as justice—never appears so triumphant, as when qualified—with clemency and mercy—I—shall not inflict any
corporal punishment on you, as this is the first offence.—But my sentence is
—that you are pecunarily punished by paying the costs—of this prosecution
—and for the future behave better.

ATTICUS. Refused.

JUSTICE. Obdurate yet I see—it was my compassion and lenity that forgave you.

ATTICUS. Then you may substitute severity or cruelty—I will pay no costs.

JUSTICE. Your provocation will oblige me to send you to goal.

ATTICUS. If your Worship durst, you would have long agone.

JUSTICE. Your insolence so far exceeds my patience that I cannot bear you
any longer in my sight. Get home about your business—but if I hear the least
complaint I shall send for you again.

THIS COURT IS DISSOLVED.

NOTES

1. Sir Edward Coke (1552–1634), author of *Institute of the Laws of England,* the first volume being known as *Coke Upon Littleton* (Chief Justice of North Wales). (ed.)

2. *Hudibras,* 1764, Part II, Canto II, ll. 235–246; ll. 239–240 omitted:
   And yet the actions be contrary,
   Just as the saints and wicked vary. (ed.)

3. Matthew, 5:28.

THE BATTLE OF BROOKLYN

A Farce in Two Acts

As it was performed on
LONG ISLAND
On Tuesday the 27th Day of August, 1776.
By the Representatives of the Tyrants of
AMERICA

Assembled at Philadelphia

For as a Flea, that goes to bed
Lies with his tail above his head:
So in this mongrel State of ours,
The rabble are the supreme powers;
Who've hors'd us on their backs, to shew us
A jadish trick, at last, and throw us.

HUDIBRAS.

NEW YORK:

Printed for J. Rivington, in the Year of
Rebellion, 1776

DRAMATIS PERSONAE

MEN

WASHINGTON,
PUTNAM,
SULLIVAN,
STIRLING,
} Rebel Chiefs

LASHER, a *Shoemaker* of New York
CLARK, a *Retailer of Rum* in Connecticut
REMSEN, a *Farmer* of New Town Long Island
} Colonels.

EBENEZER SNUFFLE, a New England *Parson, Chaplain to General Putnam.*
JOE-KING, *Servant* to Stirling.
NOAH, *Servant* to Sullivan.
SKINNER, a *Thief* employed by Putnam.

WOMEN

LADY GATES.
BETTY, *her Servant.*

OFFICERS AND SOLDIERS

SCENE: Partly within the Rebel Lines at *Brooklyn* and partly at *Gwanas.**

* The ground for this battle was the Brooklyn peninsula facing the East River and lying between Wallabout Bay on the northeast and Gowanus Cove on the southwest.

ACT I.

SCENE I: *An Apartment at Brooklyn. Enter Stirling, as from his bed-room, rubbing his head.*

STIRLING. Joe! Honest Joe!—Damn the Fellow, where can this King be; [*Looking at his watch*] odss, almost twelve o'clock. [*Enter King*]

KING. Why here, my Lord—Devil damme, Sir; pray who do you damn so?

STIR. My dear Joe, the cares that distract, and split this poor head of mine—

KING. Split!—Yes, by heaven! you drank *stinkabus* enough last night, to split the head of an Indian!

STIR. Insolence!—in future know me for your master—your lord! who has the disposal of your life.

KING. I must hold a candle to this Devil. [*Aside*] My Lord, I ask your pardon; I meant no harm, but only as an old acquaintance.—You know, my Lord, I am given to joking, and you formerly encouraged me in it, when we were concerned together in the paper manufactory.

STIR. Forgive me, honest Joe—the public cares so hang upon me, that they quite destroy my constitutional good humor. The Regulars are near to us, and every moment we expect them over the hills.

KING. Your Lordship has so long and so uniformly wished to meet them, that I thought, the nearer the prospect, the better you would have been pleased. You have no doubt, my Lord, of spitting, and roasting, and pickling these red coat fellows.

STIR. We are to meet at the Church this day, to determine in council, what to do with them. I am for surrounding—surround! is the word with me; if they were twenty times the number, I say surround them all!—But these gripes, Joe, and my canteens are empty; you must procure me something for them.

KING. O Heavens, the gripes! Zounds! a puncheon of Jamaica to have the gripes. [*Aside*] I have some peach brandy, my Lord.

STIR. The best of all possible things: it so admirably fits a man for the cabinet and the field. [*A knocking at the door*] What can that mean; run, Joe, and see who knocks.

KING. I go, Sir. [*As he goes he observes Stirling's countenance*] Pale and trembling, by that august body the Congress. [*Aside and exit*]

STIR. These bloody fellows, I fear, are in motion. I hope to God that damn'd rascal King will be shot; he has been my evil genius, ever since I was concerned with him in counterfeiting paper currency. [*Enter King*] Dear Joe, what is the matter?

KING. Nothing, but to desire you to meet the other Generals in council, two hours hence, at the church.

STIR. O, is that all; I shall attend; in the meantime, go to the Commissary of Rum, and get my canteens filled, and by all means, my good Joe, be at home when I return. [*Exit Stirling*]

KING. Canteens filled—and then thy whole soul will be in thy canteens. That is, if he has credit enough with the Commissary, to get his canteens filled with rum, he will belch it out of his stomach in the damn'dest lies, that ever disqualified a man for the character of a gentleman: and yet parson McWorther bellows from his pulpit, that this most *ignobleman,* is a chosen vessel, to execute the Lord's work.—Ill-fated country! when will this delusion end? [*Exit*]

SCENE II: *The Scene changes to a small House, in a Field: Cattle and Horses grazing. Enter LASHER[1] and CLARK.*

CLARK. Behold, Colonel, these flocks and herds; with the sword of Gideon have I made them mine; and honestly collected them, in the district allotted to me by our agreement.

LASHER. I rejoice with you in the acquisition. My harvest from the Wallabocht is like the miraculous draught:—two hundred and seven head of horned beasts, and thirty-seven horses, graze where my guards direct.

CLARK. Favour has not been so amply manifested unto me; for from the farthest verge of Gwanas, even from Caspar's house, till you come to Brewer's mills, one hundred and nine horned, and twenty-eight beasts of burthen, were all I could collect: nor was there compassion in my soul to spare one of the Kine for milk, to the offspring of a people who believe that men cannot be saved by faith alone, without works.

LASH. Impious and blasphemous tenet; destructive of Republicanism and intoleration. I doubt whether such people should be spared from the sword. —But, brother Clark, to secure what we have thus obtained by a strong hand, and mighty arm, was assigned to your care and prudence.

CLARK. That I am not unworthy of the trust, you are to know, that nine of our sloops will, this day, be discharged from the continental service: to-morrow, they will be ready at the ferry to receive the spoil. Every fifth beast, by lot, is to be the wages of their safe delivery, at New Haven, in Connecticut, the residence of the faithful. But, we being fellow laborers, if you approve—Tabitha, the wife of my bosom, shall be charged with the care of your cattle.

LASH. Be it as thou hast said; at her hands will I require them; and as I had allotted to myself a large brass Kettle, in a former division of the spoil, with the Cattle let it be convey'd, as a testimony of the love I bear unto her.

CLARK. What ever is in thy heart to do, that do and prosper. I hear that twelve thousand are to keep the hills to-day; spies proclaim some motion in the camp of the Philistians.

LASH. What the end of these things will be, I know not; but as my soul liveth I mean not to budge a jot beyond the summit of the hill, keeping in full view and practible acquisition, the fort called Green.[2]

CLARK. Know you not, the wise determination of the Congress on that head; stimulated thereto, by the prudence of our Generals; who, I do believe, received it by inspiration?

LASH. Ignorant have I been kept; but unfold the mighty tydings, for I already perceive they are big with joy.

CLARK. Have you not observed, with what address the southern militias are drawn hither?

LASH. That they are here I know, but am yet to learn the secret cause, if any secret cause there be.

CLARK. Know, then, that the Marylanders, Pennsylvanians, and the rife regiments, are mostly composed of *Europeans;* a great majority of which are Irish and Germans.

LASH. These things I am no stranger to but still lack information.

CLARK. Which way soever the battle tends, the burthen and heat of it will be theirs; for thus it is resolved, to spare the *natives,* and make no account of the *expenditure* of the *Europeans;* feel you not the power of inspiration now?

LASH. Wonderful! truly wonderful workings of wisdom indeed!

CLARK. But for some twenty head of cattle, the gleanings of Gwanas, in the orchard of one Bergen, I would not go so far: these once obtained, we will be near each other. [*Enter REMSEN,*[3] *without a hat, his hair on end; his coat torne, and every mark of fear about him*]

LASH. Mercy! mercy! O Lord, where are they?

CLARK. O heavens! he is wounded and out of his senses! Dear Colonel, can you speak.

REM. Oh! Heere Godt! what merciful scape I get this time.—Shentle-men, have you seen my *regment?*

CLARK. No, where did you leave it?—Lord help us! how near is the enemy?

REM. O Godt! O Godt! O Godt!—Count the bloodt out of me in any place.

LASH. Blood, no; nor can I see any body coming after you: your hurt, I fancy, is fear! Colonel; and your wound must be sought for in your breeches! but compose yourself, and tell us what has happened.

REM. Well, I will tell you, then. I was, yust now, van the head of regiment, close up behind *Shon van Dinen's* field. I keep my eye on *Arian Morte's* lane. I see, yust by the ground, something creep: I say my regiment, take care of yourself boys. I peep again mit both mine eyes, and see nothing: I say, boys, 'tis close up with us now—they begin for to run; my horse he see the danger too, and carry me off: Godt knows I get here; I believe the rest is all killed, or taken prisoners. [*Enter an Officer*] Godt bless you ayndant, where is the regiment?

OFF. Where! damn them, scattered in every cover between this and the place where you started.

REM. Heere Godt! all killed?

OFF. Killed! no, nor any of them hurt except four or five that you rode over: why there was not a regular within a mile, when you took fright.

LASH. O you ungodly coward! out from the presence of the brave. [*Kicks him off, and exit after him*]

OFF. That fellow kicks as awkward, as if he soon expected the same discipline: but I will go and try if possible, to collect our heroes. [*Exit Officer*]

CLARK. What credulous stuff, these *New Yorkers* are made of. The bill of lading for the cattle and horses will be in my name only: Poor Lasher! not a hide of them shalt thou have to put a stich in:—and then there is the Kettle, too! a! ha! ha! [*Exit laughing*]

SCENE III: *A Room at Brooklyn Ferry. Enter LADY GATES and BETTY.*

BETTY. After Council, Mem, General Washington will wait of you; till then he begs your patience, as the time is near when he is to meet the rest of the Generals.

LADY G. Council! a pretty collection of Councillors, indeed; but since it must be so, you shall comply with your promise to me, girl, by giving me the narrative of Harrison and your General: it will beguile the time.

BETTY. La, mem, you so discomfit me by claiming this promise, that I am a blush all over.

LADY G. Why, Betty, you must have assumed the blushing trade lately, it was not always so with you.

BETTY. Indeed your Ladyship does not make proper allowances for necessity and inexperience—Fifty dollars, and hard ones too with a promise of fifty times as much was irresistable: but Oh! the nasty beast! I almost puke at the recollection.

LADY G. Oh! that must be affectation, for bless me what could raise such ideas?

BETTY. Why, he is such a slobbering, odious, unsavory smelling creature, that I wonder any woman in the world could sleep at night, by his side.

LADY G. And yet you see, that fifty hard dollars, made you put up for a night with all the inconveniency of bad smells.

BET. A night! your Ladyship wrongs me very much: why he snored within an hour! and the first snore was signal for my retreat. I am sure, I should have been a corps, if I had been obliged to stay the night.

LADY G. Fifty dollars is a good deal of money, Betty; but did he make no claim upon you afterwards?

BET. Indeed, mem, he stayed from Congress on purpose to tease me: why he cry'd and said he was in liquor that night, and did every thing, I think, that could make me despise him, but all would not do.

LADY G. And there your affairs ended with Harrison, did they not, Betty?

BET. Not quite, my Lady; for when he found that I could not abide him, he proposed to introduce General Washington to me. The General was a very pretty Gentleman, and I consented to it on purpose to get rid of Harrison.

LADY G. This I should have imagined a favorable change myself, Betty, was it not.

BET. The General is the sweetest, meekest, melancholy fighting Gentleman; and then he is such a warrior—O mem, I shall always love the General.

LADY G. And among his other qualifications, the most liberal.

BET. Why, my Lady, I will tell you honestly: his Excellency gave me a thirty dollar bill; he assured me it would have been more, but that he was obliged to repay Harrison the fifty hard dollars that he had given me: now, mem, is not Harrison a dirty fellow in every shape that you can view him?

LADY G. No great things, girl, to be sure, from your account of him; neither is your meek, melancholy hero, from my own observation.

BET. Lord!—lord!—mem, did he not make codfish of them all at Boston! And has he not seen tory men rid upon rails at New York by the tailors and cobblers of the town! And more, my lady, did he not order the King's statue to be pulled down, and the head cut off![4] for God's sake, mem, what would you have of a hero?

LADY G. *Codfish at Boston!* it is really an odd term, Betty: but he did no more than that old fool Putnam would have done: his not forbidding that insult to humanity, at New York, was countenancing an act of barbarism; and none, but a little minded barbarian would have suffered the Arts to be trampled under foot, as he did, in the case of the King's statue.

BET. You know of these things best, mem, to be sure: but I have heard the New England officers say that he should be their General no longer than he pleased them, and may be, they would have it so.

LADY G. Be assured, girl, that if he had native dignity of heart, he would have soon convinced the rabble, that they must be governed by him, notwithstanding that he may have obtained his power by an usurpation from themselves—but hark! what clamorous noise is that in the street? Run and learn. [*Exit Betty*] There appears to be some commotion, and it grows late; I begin to despair of seeing the General. [*Enter Betty*]

BET. O, my lady, do not let us wait to see the General. The New England Colonels are in a mutiny and say they will not fight, if the boats are not all ready to carry their men off to New York, when they run away: let us go, dear mem, for I do not think we shall be safe, on this side of the Alleghany mountains.

LADY G. I will take your advice girl. O Horatio! that you should sully your laurels in the abominable cause of republican Tyrants, and Smugglers in power: to be runnagate for such miscreants, almost distracts me. [*Exeunt*]

SCENE IV: *The SCENE changes to Brooklyn Church. WASHINGTON, PUTNAM, SULLIVAN and STIRLING in Council.*

WASH. Gentlemen, spies from Flat Bush inform that the regulars are making a disposition to cross the hills, near that place.—General Putnam's wisdom in ordering that road to be flanked with breast works is now apparent. Lord Stirling, with his usual intrepidity and precision, has reconnoitered their numbers, which he finds to be about seven thousand. General Sullivan has appointed the hill with exquisite judgment; where the Brigades under him and Lord Stirling are to take post and act as occasion may require: twelve thousand men are allotted for the service of sending them back to their ships. I, with eight thousand will stay within these lines, to be called out to the slaughter and pursuit, unless our present deliberations, alter this plan of operation. My Lord, the Council expects your opinion.

Stir. I rise to give it to the most respectable and most puissant council of general officers, that this, or any other age ever produced. I would not presume Gentlemen, to speak in this place, without being conscious that I possess the energy and oratory of a *Burke!* or even write on the subject, but that I feel the powers and the pen of *Junius!* That I reconnoitered them is most true; and if my weak opinion has any weight in council I am for *surrounding* them, and when we have got them hemmed in, I am then for sending to our noble Commander in chief in these lines,—to know what to do with them.

Sul. Pompous, slimsey, drunken fool. [*Aside*] The noble Lord has said nothing against the disposition that the General had pointed out, and of which I approve.—His Lordship's ideas are exceedingly *surrounding;* I wish the practice may be as easy as the theory, and that their numbers may not exceed seven thousand:—but if the council holds the opinion of General Washington and myself, our deliberations are at an end, and we cannot be too soon at our different posts.

Put. I this morning gave the chaps another pill, and I will tell you how; you know the road to Bedford, a little on this side the house that the bandy legged Jew lived in; well, d'ye see, there is on each side the road, a stone wall, near three feet high; beyond that on each side, are clear fields—what do you think I have done there?

Stir. Why something like a great officer, nobody doubts.

Put. Swamp me, if I have not hove up a breastwork, right across the road from wall to wall,—but before we break up, determine, Gentlemen, what I am to do with my prisoners.

Stir. Right, General, I should have gone to my post, and been at a loss on this head.

Wash. Send them to me: a great part of Fort Green is allotted for their reception; but be sure that they are disarmed and well guarded.

Stir. O, to be sure, undoubtedly, Sir, we will take care of that. I am for my post: Gentlemen, farewell.

Put. A little business dispatched, and I will call upon you there. [*Exit Stirling*] If your Excellency should have any commands for me an hour hence, I may be found upon the Flat Bush road: your servant, Gentlemen. [*Exit Putnam*]

Wash. Good betide them both.—After this fustion, a little sober reasoning, General Sullivan, may fit the mind for the doubtful events of war. My apprehensions from the King's troops believe me are trifling, compared with the risque we run, from the people of America at large. The tyranny, that our accursed usurpation has made necessary, which they now feel, and feeling, I fear, will soon make them see through the disguise. Their rage no doubt will be heightened by the slaughter that will probably ensue; and we, as members of the Congress fall the first victims of it.—O Sullivan! my heart never consented to this ruin of my native country.

Sul. My dear General, the moments for reflection are elapsed, and irrecoverable. Our safety is first in conquest; if that is denied to our endeavors, I am sure we can obtain better terms from our much injured Sovereign, than from our more injured country,—but wear a less rueful countenance; it is a proverb among the troops, that their General is much melted down, since the fleet arrived.

Wash. Our soldiers are a standing miracle to me; they define sensibly upon matters that are unimportant to them, and resign their powers of thinking to us, in a case where their all is at stake; and do not yet discover, that we make them the engines of our power at the expense of all that is dear and sacred to them as men!—but avaunt reflection! Our hope, my dear Sullivan, is in you; every command of ground is ours, with a perfect knowledge of all the woods and defiles: these advantages, at the least, double the strength of our men; and if we cannot defend these, I know of no place we can.

Sul. All things that depend upon me, will, I hope meet with your approbation, and I shall aim to infuse such sentiments into the troops, that our next meeting may be ushered in with greetings of congratulation; till then, my dear General, farewell. [Exit Sullivan]

Wash. Greetings of congratulation! oh! could I congratulate myself, on finding my lost peace of mind!—on the restoration of my honor! O! cursed ambition! what have I sacrificed to thee? An ambition, too, of foreign growth; obtruded upon me by the most artful, insinuating villains, that ever enslaved a, once, free and happy country. To behold myself, against my principle and better judgment, made the tool of their diabolical determinations to entail a war upon my fellow subjects of America.—Heigho! ho! [Looking at his watch] Bless me, so late and my engagement to a lady not complied with. [Exit]

Scene V: *A Room in a House at Brooklyn. Enter PUTNAM and SNUF-FLE.*

Snuff. My dear General, the great, the important day advances; big with the fate of empire, in the United States of America.

Put.   True, good Sir: and I laugh to think, that when we have established our power, and driven these red coats into the sea, what ripping information you Gentlemen will make in church affairs. Down goes Episcopacy and Quakerism, at least. I hope you wont leave one broad-brim on the continent.

Snuff.   Why really, General, we shall be very apt to make free with those Gentlemen. We have long beheld with a jealous eye, the growing power of the Episcopal Clergy, and considered them as the only obstacle to our becoming the heads of the Church in America, a dignity which so properly belongs to the Elect, and for which they have had the assurance to contend with the Lord's own people. As for the Quakers, who in general have joined the Tories against us, we shall not fail to produce an "ancient testimony" in their behalf: I mean the testimony of our forefathers: till with fines, whipping, imprisonment, and the gallows, we have extirpated them from the face of the earth.

Put.   In the mean time, we shall not be behind hand with the Tories: for as the best estates in America belong to them, it is but cooking up some new fangled oath, which their squeamish consciences wont let them swallow; then, whip go their estates, like a juggler's ninepence, and themselves to prison, to be hanged as traitors to the commonwealth. [*Enter SKINNER*]

Snuff.   Very true, my dear General: but here comes one of your officers. I will retire, to offer up my prayers for the success of our arms, while you pursue the more important business of your department. [*Exit*]

Put.   Adieu, Sir. Well, Skinner, what news with you?

Skin.   The horses are delivered, as your Excellency directed. They are, by this time, well on their way to Connecticut; and so elegant a string of nine horses, are not to be picked up again, on all Long Island.

Put.   My letter tells me they are clever horses:—but that horse of *Polhemus*[5]—O my heart was set upon that horse: you let him slip through your fingers carelessly, Skinner: or did the owner of him tempt you with a bribe, to leave him—I wish to know where he is?

Skin.   I know where he is, to the length of my whip. I careless! I take a bribe!—why the General should know me better, the horse is at Harlem.

Put.   At Harlem!—why what notion of deviltry could send him there! Is there any body but us upon the lay, on this Island.

Skin.   What's his name brought him there—damn his name, I can't remember it; he is son however, to the Governor of Rhode Island.[6]

Put.   O ho! then I quite excuse you; you are too young in the business to be a match for young Fitch: he inherits his father's talents. I had expectation though, that we should have done better, with your knowledge of the country and other advantages;—I had reckoned upon twenty horses.

SKIN. I myself, Sir, thought that number sure, but he lay in my rear and brought off six that I had reconnoitered.

PUT. Well, Skinner, as the business is over for the present, and we expect bloody noses in a few hours, there is a hundred dollars for your encouragement. [*Gives him a handful of Congress notes*] Go over, now, and join your regiment.

SKIN. I hope your Excellency will reconsider the matter, and make it more; there is not one of those horses but that is worth more than a hundred and fifty dollars—consider, Sir!

PUT. Consider—why you are an unreasonable whelp! do you consider, that I took you from serving drams to Negroes, for your mother Foster at Rockaway and robbing the neighboring hen roosts for a livelihood! From petty larceny, you cur, I put you at the head of the procession; procured you a lieutenant's commission, and a separate command to hunt Tories on this island in order to push you forward—and dare you grumble?

SKIN. I do not grumble, but fifty dollars more would enable me to take the field with credit: it would make my regimentals my own.

PUT. I seldom mistake my men: I knew that you had talents, Skinner, or I should not have employed you; I will therefore point out a fund for you to raise the fifty dollars more. Remember, Sir, the fuzee you filched at Merrick; item, the two watches, rings &c, &c, at several other places; you gave me no account of these, though I had an equitable demand upon you for half. There is a fifty dollar fund for you,—dont you think, young man, to catch old birds with chaff. It is near night: I must to my post, and get you over the ferry to your duty. [*Exit Putnam*]

SKIN. What a damn'd old scoundrel he is: how the devil did he know of the gun and the other things?—In future I will do business for myself. [*Exit*]

ACT II.

SCENE I: *A HILL at Gwanas about two miles from Brooklyn lines, with an encampment on it. Time, about three o'clock in the morning. Enter a SOLDIER.*

SOL. Where's General Stirling?—Hollo, General Stirling!—Zounds how dark it is. [*Enter Stirling half dressed*]

STIR. For God's sake! what is the matter, sentry?

SOL. Here, Sir! it is I that call, to inform your Lordship, there has been a great deal of shooting towards the Red Lion within this little while:—there! there it begins again.

STIR. It does indeed: do you think it comes any thing nearer, sentry?

SOL. Rather nearer, if anything; though much in the same place.

STIR. Run, sentry, to the rear, make my respects to General Sullivan, and beg of him to come hither.

SOL. I will, my Lord. There it goes again; ripping work, my Lord! [*Exit Soldier*]

STIR. Now will I endeavor to get button'd up and my garters tied. [*Enter CLARK*] O Colonel Clark!—from whence are you come?

CLARK. From where our out sentries are attacked. I see you are getting ready, my Lord.

STIR. But where are they attacked? Where is the enemy? Are there many of them—are they coming forward—is any body killed, say dear Will?

CLARK. I cannot tell you half of what you have already asked me; but I will tell you all I know. They sent a Captain to relieve me: I would not be relieved by a Captain, so I went to sleep at one Bergen's, from whence the out sentries were relieved. This Bergen awaked me a while ago, and said there was shooting in his field.

STIR. God bless me! shooting in his field! was it near the house!

CLARK. Very near, so I stole out, for I knew the road dark as it was. Every thing was still, as if nothing had happened; except some groans of dying men that appeared to be at a little distance. But I have seen nothing, nor heard any thing by the way.

STIR. Then their numbers are still a secret?

CLARK. I will be bound there are not fifty of them, or there would have been some noise.

STIR. O damn it! 'tis nothing but a scouting party.—Come Colonel, we will take a whistle from my canteens.

CLARK. With all my heart, my Lord.—Poison take the canteens; I have lost the cattle that were in Bergen's orchard. [*Aside*] [*Enter five Soldiers*] What are these! who are you?

1ST SOL. We are the remains of the out post guard, your honors.

STIR. And where are the rest of the guard, my good lads.

1ST SOL. In Sarah's bosom, I hope.

2D SOL. In Abraham's bosom he means, noble General.

1ST SOL. Blood-an-oons, is not she his wife? which makes it all one.

STIR. Leave off this trifling, and tell me what you know.

1ST SOL. You honor must know, that we *was* standing by the end of a side of an Indian cornfield, up yonder a piece. We heard something rustle among the watermellon leaves, and saw something move; we bid them stand and blazed away like brave boys.

STIR. Well, my lad, and what followed?

1ST SOL. Followed! by my soul, a sharp iron thing, that they call a bayonet.

STIR. And what then?

1ST SOL. *What then!* your honor! why to be sure, the few that could run, run away; and then all was peace and quietness.

STIR. Do you not know then, how many there were?

1ST SOL. How many! your honor must know, that they were speechless; they carried their tongues in *them* damn'd bayonets, and most of our guard, I believe, are eating breakfast with their great-grand-fathers.

STIR. What corps do you belong to?

1ST SOL. Pennsylvanians, an please your honor.

STIR. Go, and join your regiment. [*Exit Soldiers*] Colonel Clark, as it begins to be light, go and get intelligence. I every moment expect General Sullivan: one or the other of us you will find here, to make a report to.

CLARK. I shall not stay long, my Lord. [*Exit Clark*]

STIR. I begin to feel easy; it has been but a scouting party; and they have gone back again. It is a devilish raw morning, and I must have something to keep the cold out. [*Exit*]

SCENE II: *A HILL, with troops drawn up, under arms. Time, broad day-light. Enter SULLIVAN and STIRLING.*

STIR. Well, do you not think, from the examination of these fellows, that it was a mere scouting party that surprized the guard?

SUL. Their silence, my Lord, with me, marks order and good conduct:

besides they do not make war by scouting parties—but here comes Colonel Clark. [*Enter Clark*]

CLARK. Gentlemen, the regulars are in motion: they are numerous, and will be here within an hour. From yonder hill, I looked down upon them.

STIR. Good Colonel, have they any artillery with them?

CLARK. I know not, my Lord; but I must away and join my men. O what a scrape those cattle have brought me into. I am afraid I shall be obliged to fight at last. [*Aside and exit*]

SUL. Well, my Lord, will you make a disposition for your favorite scheme of surrounding?

STIR. For God's sake, dear General, don't mention it, I did not expect them this way. Our whole dependance is upon you, my dear General; but do not let them cut off our retreat.

SUL. Let your brigades immediately take post in the bottom, and extend from the small house below, as far as the stone house upon the left; and farther, if the hill gives them cover: let them approach as near the road as possible, without being discovered. The Pennsylvanians are to draw up, at the foot of this hill, in full view of the enemy. From their uniform they may be taken for Hessians; and the fire from the brigades be more completely surprizing and effectual.

STIR. It shall be done. Oh! it shall be done. [*Exit Stirling*]

SUL. If they should force these brigades to the hill, we can easily maintain this post, against the united force of Britain, without loss: and make the retreat to our lines, when we please unmolested. [*Re-enter STIRLING*]

STIR. The Brigades are disposed, as your Excellency directed; and the regulars are nearly up to them; you will see their advanced guard pass the stone house, directly.

SUL. There they are, and have discovered the Pennsylvanians for they have quited the road, and push towards them.

STIR. I hope to God they will push back again, as soon as our fire begins. O! there they go—well fired my boys! they cannot stand this! you'll see, they will push directly, General.

SUL. I see they do push, but it is with their bayonets, and our men are scampering towards us. [*Enter a Pennsylvanian, hastily*] Stop, soldier, you are far enough.

PEN. I will be judge of that, my dear; for by my soul, honey, you have brought old Ireland about your ears, at last; and we can find the way to eat iron without asking such vermine as you for victuals. [*Exit*]

STIR. Dear General, what shall we do now?

SUL. Ply the artillery as far as possible. [*Enter an Officer*]

OFF. Towards the south, an incessant firing has prevailed for half an hour, nor has it ought approached: my post is that way advanced, but I thought my duty bid me quit it, to give you this information.

SUL. You have my thanks. To your post again, and let me be speedily informed, if the firing approaches. [*Exit Officer*] While they are kept at bay, my Lord, we are safe upon this hill.

STIR. But yet we should prepare for a retreat—for see, where they fearless climb up yonder hill.

SUL. There is nothing to obstruct us in our rear, my Lord; we will retreat in good time. [*Enter CLARK*]

CLARK. Lost! O Lord! undone! ruined! destroyed!

SUL. Amazement! what ails the man?

CLARK. In the rear—there in our rear—no retreat! no retreat!

SUL. Too true—there is part of the royal army, indeed, between us and our lines.

STIR. O General Sullivan! General Sullivan! what do you think of it now?

SUL. This I now know, my Lord, that we heaven-born Generals are exceedingly apt to lead our troops, to the devil.

STIR. But my dear General, what shall we do?

SUL. Just what you please, every man is now his own General, so Gentlemen farewell. [*Exit*]

STIR. Do not leave me also, Colonel Clark. O Lord, incline their hearts to mercy.

CLARK. Amen, and amen. I hope, however, we are not of consequence to be hanged. This way, my Lord, this way.

SCENE III: *FORT GREEN, in Brooklyn Lines: A Centinel on one of the Merlins,* looking out. Enter WASHINGTON.*

WASH. What do you look so earnestly at, Sentry?

CEN. At our people, Sir, that are setting fire to the houses and barns in their retreat.

WASH. What, are they retreating then?

CEN. Look this way, Sir; there they run like so many deer, and will get in: but the poor souls yonder, that come across the meadow, and attempt to cross the mill creek; O, what a number of them stick in the mud, and the stronger ones make a bridge of them.

WASH. All other retreat must be cut off; but I shall soon know the event,

---

* A kind of canon.

for there comes Putnam galloping. [*Enter PUTNAM*] What is the disaster? What news do you bring me, General Putnam.

PUT. This is no Boston work, Sir; they are in earnest! Orders must be immediately issued for the boats to be in readiness to carry our people over to New York.

WASH. There is time enough for that, General Putnam, after we have defended these works; the account of the Battle is what I wish to hear.

PUT. Defend, Sir! we cannot defend these works; our people won't defend them; if they do not see the boats, they will swim over, they won't be hemmed in to be made minc'd of. If you don't give your orders, I will give the orders myself.

WASH. If it must be so, the orders shall originate with me; and as soon as you have satisfied me on the fate of the day, proper measures shall be taken.

PUT. Accursed fate, indeed, and most impious, for they took us fasting; and then they deceived us—a most devilish deception too; for they did not come any one way that we had marked out for them.

WASH. Well, but you had the woods, and the hills, and every other advantage. The riflemen did great execution from behind the trees, surely!

PUT. Zounds! Sir, the regulars did all the execution! They know that rifle-men are deer killers!—Rifle guns and rifle frocks, will be as cheap in their camp to-morrow, as cods heads in New Foundland.—But the orders, Sir; there is no time to be lost; they are at our heels.

WASH. Have patience, General. What is our loss? Where are the other Generals?

PUT. How can I tell, where they are, or what our loss really is; but I am sure it is thousands. Good God, Sir, let us make haste to save what is not lost.

WASH. This, General Putnam, is against my will; but I wait on you to execute yours. [*Exeunt*]

SCENE IV: *A Room at Brooklyn Ferry. Enter NOAH, Solus, his clothes covered with creek mud.*

NOAH. Notwithstanding your dirty condition, Mr. Noah, I congratulate you on your safe arrival into your old quarters; neither hol'd by musquet balls, nor swelled up with salt water and creek mud. Thanks to my activity that I am not crabs meat with the rest. [*Enter KING*] Welcome, Joe; dripping from the creek, I see; but I am glad to see you alive!

KING. Confirm it, that I am really alive, for I feel some doubts about it.

No. Don't you know me, then?

KING. As well as I know myself, Noah; but are we not both in the other world.

No. Why, man, look about you; and you will find this to be the very room that we have inhabited for some time past.

KING. My senses, good Noah, claim conviction: something, first, to cherish me, and then I may be convinced, that I can, with propriety, talk upon sublunary subjects.

No. Behold, Joe, this pocket bottle; one-half of its contents, I prescribe to your conviction and restoration.

KING. [Drinks] Now I return your congratulations, and am heartily glad to find you on this side of the grave—but, Noah, what has become of our Generals?

No. Killed or taken prisoners; but I suppose the latter. My poor General, I quite lament him.

KING. Mine is under the same predicament, but I have not a pity for him: —nor should I love you very much, if I thought you serious in your lamentation.

No. Consider; he and I were brought up together: we went together to sea before the mast, and since he commenced lawyer, he maintained a suit for me against my mother, and got the cause.

KING. Confound the dog! But was he really a lawyer, and did he influence you, to commence an action against your mother?

No. He!—why, that fellow, drank flip every night with the common people of our town of Berwick, and had art enough, to influence them to all his ends.

KING. And some hundreds of the common people has he influenced to their end, this day. But, for God's sake, Noah, how came a man of your understanding, in the capacity of this fellow's servant?

No. Without doubt, I might have started with a regiment, and probably, have been, myself, a general by this time. But I saw through their, topsy-turvey schemes;—though I was obliged to float with the tide, I knew the post of honor would be the most private station. But Sullivan will be a loss to his family.

KING. So will not Stirling. He will be a loss to no body but those that find him. Had Sullivan any property?

No. Most excellent property, for he made a property of weakness and ignorance, and consequently had an extensive fund.—But yours was a titled general, and I suppose very full of property; as he has often declared he was of principle.

KING. His principle, Noah, has for years past, been to withhold other people's property from them; and when all the resources of art failed, his estate was exposed to sale by virtue of an execution: But he resisted the

Sheriff, and declared himself a partizan of confusion because law and order, would compel him to acts of justice.—But do you recollect, that this is the fast day?

No. Is it really! then it is one of the baits, which the Continental Congress threw out, for the people of America to bite at; and the event gives the lie to the inflaming and prophetic oratory, this day resounded from the pulpits of New England. A day, on which, Heaven has discarded them and disavowed their cause, in a remarkable manner. O King, our preachers prevented this unhappy dispute from coming to a bloodless issue.

KING. It is a maxim with the Congress at Philadelphia that by the marvellous, the vulgar are to be robb'd of their reason; but heaven has rejected the sacrifice, that the people may open their eyes, and be no longer the dupes of their tyranny, deception and bloodshed.

No. From the first meeting of that *Hydra* at Philadelphia, its sixty-four mouths, have all been open to devour two strangers!

KING. Devouring mouths, I know they are; but what strangers do you point at.

No. Power! and Riches!

KING. True, very true—strangers indeed to most of them: the first they have amply usurped from the people, and have art enough to make use of them as instruments, to confirm the usurpation.

No. They are indeed, such monopolizers of liberty, that they do not suffer other people to follow their inclinations: but as we know and consequently detest their machinations; let us avail ourselves of the character of servants, and the confusion of retreat to lie concealed, until they are clear of the Island.

KING. Agreed; and in order that we may claim the mercy that our good old master has extended to his erring servants, and return to that authority which never oppressed a subject; let us renew our allegiance to the most admirable and virtuous Prince that ever swayed sceptre; and join our weak endeavors, in supporting a constitution, that has been, at once, the envy and admiration of the whole world.

No. I honor your sentiments because I experimentally know them to be just. And O! almighty disposer of human events, open the eyes of my deluded fellow subjects, in this, once, happy country: encourage them to a free exercise of that reason, which is the portion of every individual, that each may judge for himself: then peace and order will smile, triumphant, over the rugged face of war and horror; the same hand that sows shall reap the field; and our vines and vineyards shall be our own. [*Exeunt omnes*]

THE END

NOTES

1. In mid-June, 1776, Col. Lasher of the Rebel Army, an ex-shoemaker, led a mob in pursuit of Tories whom he then rode on a rail.

2. Fort Greene, a redoubt about the center of the Continental lines.

3. Abraham Remsen, a Dutchman, was a farmer from the Gowanus area of Brooklyn.

4. Incidents based on fact.

5. Rev. John T. Polhemus of the Reformed Church in America preached at Flat Bush, Long Island, 1754–76.

6. Perhaps there is some confusion here. Thomas Fitch, Governor of Connecticut from 1754 to 1766 was outspoken in his reaction to the Intolerable Acts.

DARBY'S RETURN

A Comic Sketch

As Performed at the New-York Theatre,
November, 24, 1789
For the Benefit of Mr. Wignell

Written by William Dunlap

NEW-YORK

Printed by Hodge, Allen, and Campbell
And Sold at their respective Bookstores
and by Berry and Rogers

M.DCC.LXXXIX

CHARACTERS

Darby

Dermot

Clown

Father Luke

Old Woman

Kathleen

This play is reprinted courtesy of the New York Public Library, Astor, Lenox, and Tilden Foundations.

SCENE: *The Village of Carton. After some airs from the Poor Soldier, the curtain draws, and discovers Darby, surrounded by Father Luke, Dermot, Kathleen, and villagers—They huzza and advance.*

AIR—"What True Felicity."

FATHER LUKE.	Come neighbours come, come, all around me come,
	    Let's welcome home,
	    This silly loon,
	    That's wandering been,
	    Thro' many a scene,
	And left his own village to mourn him.

KATHLEEN.	Now Darby we're glad to see you,
	Good wishes have ever been wi' you,
	    Since Dermot is mine,
	    My friendship is thine;
	No longer good Darby I'll flout you.

CHORUS OF VILLAGERS.	Now Darby we're glad to see you, Good wishes have ever been wi' you, Now where have you been? And what have you seen? I prythee good fellow now tell us?
FATHER LUKE.	Now Darby let's hear of the many scars, You got in wars; The man who dares In battle to mix, 'Tis seven to six, But he'd make a good sieve ever after.

DARBY.	Oh trust me no bit of a wound, sir,
	O'er Darby's whole carcase is found, sir;
	    He doesn't know fear—
	    But he never could bear,
	To dirty good cloaths on the ground, sir.

CHORUS OF VILLAGERS.	Now Darby we're glad to see you,
	Good wishes have ever been wi' you,
	    Now where have you been?
	    And what have you seen?

	I prythee good fellow now tell us!
DARBY.	I prythee good people now stand away—
	Make room I pray!
	Hear what I say—
	I'll tell you such feats,
	In colds and in heats,
	As will make ye all gape 'till ye choak, sirs.
	Now neighbours stand off; pray don't crowd so,
	And what need ye all gabble loud so,
	Who the devil can speak,
	While ye cackle and squeak,
	Like so many geese in a hog-style.
CHORUS OF VILLAGERS.	Now Darby we're glad to see you;
	Good wishes have ever been wi' you;
	Now where have you been?
	And what have you seen?
	I prythee good fellow now tell us!

[Music ceases]

DARBY. *[Advancing]*   Now! give me room to breathe; there! stand away;
All form a ring, and then we'll see fair play.
You—

OLD WOMAN.   *Darby,* I'm deaf, and must nearer come.
DARBY.   If you would hear good dame, you must be dumb.
You all remember, neighbours, ah! too well,
(Tho' faith! full cheery I'll the story tell.)
How I was jilted by this gypsy here—[*To Kathleen*]
Never tight Irish boy sure, felt so queer:
Then *Pat* must come too, with his "row de dow,"
So, for a gen'ral's staff I sold my plough,
My *bald fac'd Robin,* and my *brindled Cow;*
Then off to Dublin, joy, I nimbly pack,
And there I play'd a game at paddy wack:
Oh, to be sure, I didn't flash at all!
I didn't dance a little at the ball!
But having spent my cash—for cash will go!
FATHER LUKE.   Ah, Darby! that's a truth we all well know!

DARBY.
Sure I Resolv'd for London; aye my boys!
When I took leave we made a glorious noise!

OLD WOMAN.
Good souls! shed tears so, ha?

DARBY.
Tears, mother! no,
We nothing shed but whiskey:—Off I go!
Pop board a ship—fuddled—mistook my way;
And when I come to rub my eyes next day,
Was on my way to *Dantzick:* Silly loon!—

OLD WOMAN.
Poor Darby! taken *sea sick* too, so soon!

CLOWN.
Oh, *Darby,* did you ever see a whale?

DERMOT.
Hush, neighbours, hush, let *Darby* tell his tale.

DARBY.
Well, see me landed; sure, without a farthing,
So, Prussian hero turn'd, to keep from starving;
Drill'd, drub'd and basted, curst and kick't and fisted,
My nice shock golden hair, black't, greas'd & twisted;
I'm sure wonder how it ever come
To bring its own dear carrot-colour home;
So close screw'd up,—sure, *Dermot,* you would think,
My skin like drum-head tight:—I couldn't wink;
Loaded with belts and buckles at all points,
We mov'd like wooden men with iron joints.
—But merit can't be hid:—I soon was rais'd.

OLD WOMAN.
Aye, aye, I warrant, goodness now be prais'd!

FATHER LUKE.
What, to a Halbert? Thirteen-pence a day?

DARBY.
No, to three halberts;—cat-o-nine-tail pay;
There I was sav'd by little *Captain Pat,*
And where d'ye think I went to after that?
To Austria, my lads! and there I swagger'd,
Strutted & puff'd, look'd big, drank hard & stagger'd,
While my great master, doing much the same,
Bully'd the Dutchman—thus we play'd the game;
Till the curst Turks, those whisker'd, sabred dogs,
Men-eating Hannibals, with hearts like logs,

Made war upon us; then I thought 'twas best,
To seek an army that was more at rest;
Not that I minded fighting: Not a button!
(For some may think I meant to save my mut-
ton:)
No, no!—But being taught by *Father Luke,*
That Turks are heretics, I wisely took
Precautions not to have my morals hurt,
By any intercourse with such vile dirt:
So finding this was not the place for me,
Once more, good neighbours, I embark'd for
sea.

KATHLEEN.   Alas! what hardships 'twas your lot to prove.
DARBY.   Yes, Kathleen, yes! and all for sake of love.
              Now on the waves again, with swelling sail—
CLOWN.   Do, *Darby,* tell me!—Did you see a whale?
DARBY.   Whales! Aye, yes—thick as hops—since you
              must know,
              Dancing Scotch reels—two thousand strong or
              so.
CLOWN.   Oh marcy!
OLD WOMAN.   Gooddy!
CLOWN.   Odds bobs sningers.
OLD WOMAN.   Oh!
DARBY.   Well neighbours, now by destinies and fates,
              See me safe landed in the United States;
              And now I'm at the best part of my story,
              For there poor Darby was in all his glory;
              From north to south, where ever I appear'd,
              With deeds and words, my spirits oft they
              cheer'd;
              But more especially I lik'd to work,
              At one nice little place they call'd New-York;
              Oh, there they lov'd me dearly, never fear
              But Darby loves them too, with heart sincere.
              There too I saw some mighty pretty shows;
              A revolution without blood or blows;
              For as I understood the cunning elves,
              The people all revolted from themselves;
              Then after joining in a kind of consession,

They all agreed to walk in a procession;
So turners, taylors, tinkers, tavern-keepers,
With parsons, blacksmiths, lawyers, chimney
sweepers,
All neatly dress'd, and all in order fair,
Nice painted standards, waving in the air,
March'd thro' the town—eat beef—and
drank strong beer.
Soon after that I saw another show,
A man who'd fought to free the land from
woe,
Like me had left his *farm* a *soldiering* to go;
But having gain'd his point, he had, *like me,*
Return'd his own *potatoe ground* to see;
But there he couldn't rest;—with one accord
He's call'd to be a kind of—, not a Lord—
I don't know what—he's not a great man, sure,
For poor men love him, just as he was poor!
They love him like a father or a brother.

DERMOT.   As we poor Irishmen love one another.
DARBY.   Just so.
FATHER LUKE. Why that's the strangest sight of all.
KATHLEEN.   How look'd he, Darby? Was he short or tall?
DARBY.   Why sure I didn't see him: to be sure,
As I was looking hard from out the door,
I saw a man in regimentals fine,
All lace and glitter, bother'um and shine;
And so I look'd at him, till all was gone,
And then, I found that he was not the one.
By this time, boys, I wanted to get home;
I thought you would be glad to see me come;
So, as I've often heard the people say,
The farthest round is much the shortest way,
I went to France. I always did love quiet,
And there I got in the middle of a riot.
There they cried *"viva la nation," "liberty,"*
And all the *bag and tails* swore they'd be free;
They caught the fire quite across the ocean,
And to be sure, they're in a nice commotion:
(Down with the bastile—tuck up the jailor.

Cut off my lor's head, then pay his taylor.)
Oh bless their hearts, if they can but get free,
They'll soon be as fat and as jolly as we;
Some took the *liberty* to plunder others,
Because equality is more like brothers.
You may be sure I didn't stay there long.
So here I am, boys, hearty hale and strong!
But oh, New-York's the place to get a wife,
Aye, that's the place to lead a merry life.

FATHER LUKE. Why, Darby, boy, why didn't you stay there?
DARBY. Because I wish'd to pay a visit here;
To see how all the *Carton* lasses thrive,
And ask ye, sure, if ye are all alive.
But I'll go back again, oh never fear!
I'll not be after leaving them, my dear:
You will not catch me staying a great while,
From where I'm never seen without a smile.
Oh may their little country ever prove,
The land of liberty and seat of love.
Oh bless their little hearts, and all they've got,
And they may soon *have* all that they *have not*.

CLOWN. Well, Darby, but did you see nothing more?
Didst see no Indians?
DARBY. Indians?—By the score.
I saw balloons too, and I learn'd a song;
I'll sing it t'ye—it isn't very long.

AIR—"The Taylor done over."

I.

We had a balloon there, as big as a church, sirs,
And when it went off we were left in the lurch, sirs;
For while we were watching, like sportsmen for plover,
The linen took fire—and did us all over.

Over, over, oh!

II.

Oh when we look'd up and saw nothing but smoke, sirs;
We all of us laugh'd;—tho' none found out the joke, sirs,

Then all in a flock, like before-mentioned plover,
We sneak'd into town;—very fairly done over.

Over, over, oh!

III.

Thus Darby his travels, has briefly related,
And all his adventures, in due order stated:
And as he has prov'd, that of truth he's a lover,
He hopes the *pit critics*—will not do him over.

Over, over, oh!

IV.

He looks to the *boxes,* in hopes to find favour,
He's a tight Irish boy—tho' of clownish behaviour;
Let the ladies remember, love made him a rover,
And they can't have the heart, sure—to do Darby over.

Over, over, oh!

V.

You jolly round faces, poor Darby's long lov'd you,

[To the gallery]

Your applause he may hope since he often has prov'd you:
May you ne'er want for *fun,* while you're here under cover,
And the fiddles still play you—the Taylor done over.

Over, over, oh!

VI.

Your healths will he drink, in a cup of brown nappy,

[All around]

May the single be married, the married be happy:
And as gratitude many great failings may cover,
Darby's heart shall be grateful—*till death does him over.*

Over, over, oh!

THE END

PO-CA-HON-TAS

or, THE GENTLE SAVAGE

IN TWO ACTS

by John Brougham, Esq.

An Original
Aboriginal Erratic Operatic Semi-Civilized and
Demi-Savage Extravaganza, being a Per-Version of Ye Trewe
and Wonderrefulle Hystorie of Ye Rennownned
Princesse.

The MUSIC Dislocated and Re-set by James G. Maeder, M. D.; and presented to
Public Notice through the INSTRUMENTALITY of SIGNOR LA MANNA. The SCENERY
painted from daguerreotypes and other authentic documents by Mr. H. ISHER-
WOOD, greatly assisted by his own vivid imagination and Mr. WALLACE. The
COSTUMES cut from the original plates, and thoroughly digested, by Mr. T. FLAN-
NERY, and several auxiliary thimble-riggers. The MACHINERY, Wings, Flies, and
other Entomologia, by Mr. DEMILT, and various other philosophers. The CON-
SIDERABLE PROPERTIES, crowns, sceptres, war-clubs, Indian pipes, and other regalia,
by Mr. TIMMANY, and his aids.

Reprinted from the Acting Edition published by Samuel French.

DRAMATIS PERSONAE

CAPTAIN JOHN SMITH. The undoubted Original, vocal and instrumental, in the settlement of Virginia, in love with Pocahontas, according to *this* story, though somewhat at variance with *his* story. ....MR. WALCOT.

LIEUT. THOMAS BROWN. Second in Command, a hitherto neglected Genius, whose claims on posterity are now for the first time acknowledged, as is but right. ....MR. BARRY.

WILLIAM JONES. Sometimes called Bill, another of the same sort left.

MR. SIMPSON.

MYNHEER ROLFF. The real Husband of Pocahontas, but dramatically divorced contrary to all law and fact. ....MR. PETERS.

BENJAMIN BRACE. ⎤ Splicers of main braces, shiverers of timbers, anathe-
JOHN JUNK. ⎟ matizers of eyes and limbs, promiscuously general
HENRY HALYARD. ⎬ dealers in single combats and double hornpipes, and
WILLIAM BUNTLINE. ⎟ altogether, amazingly nautical people. .....MESSRS.
BARNABAS BINNACLE. ⎦   HARE, THOMPSON, JOHNS, REDDY, JAMES.

H. J. POW-HA-TAN I. King of the Tuscaroras—a crotchetty Monarch, in fact, a Semi-Brave ....MR. BROUGHAM.

THE RIGHT HON. QUASH-AL-JAW, Speaker of the Savage House of Lords. Straightener of unpleasant kinks, and oiler of troubled waters, unraveller of knotty points, adjuster of pugnacious difficulties, and Grand Eye Parliamentary Factotum and Fugleman. ....MR. BURKE.

O-PO-DIL-DOC. One of the Aboriginal F. F. V's, an indignant dignitary.
MR. LEVERE.

COL-O-GOG. Another warm-hearted and headed Son of Old Virginia the untiring. ....MR. STODDART.

JIN-GO, Sergeant at Arms. A Friend to swear by. ....MR. JEFFRIES.

KREEM-FAY-SLOON. Bearer of Dispatches, and news carrier in ordinary.
MR. HARRISON.

Ip-Pah-Kak.
Sas-Sy-Pril.
Kod-Liv-Royl. } Medicine Men, of the Saultz and Senna-ca Tribe. { MR. OLIVER.
MR. SAMUELS.
MR. REYNOLDS.
Kal-O-Mel. } MR. CARVER.

H.R.H. Princess Po-Ka-Hon-Tas. The Beautiful, and very properly un-dutiful daughter of King Pow-Ha-Tan, married, according to the ridiculous dictum of actual circumstance, to Master Rolff, but the author flatters himself much more advantageously disposed of in the Acting edition.

MISS HODSON.

Poo-Tee-Pet. } Interesting offshoots from aristocratic stock { MRS. STEPHENS.
Di-Mun-Di. } anterior to the First Families in Virginia { MRS. CONVERS.

Wee-Cha-Ven-Da. } Embodying the rigid principles of the Tuscarora Fashionable Finishing School { MRS. SYLVESTER.
Kros-As-Kan-Bee. } MRS. THOMPSON.

Dah-Lin-Duk.
O-You-Jewel.
Luv-Lie-Kreeta. } Their "dear charges," for whom they don't forget to charge dear enough for in the Quarterly Bills. { MISS MELVILLE.
MISS THOMPSON.
MISS PINE.
Oso-Char-Ming. } MISS CARMAN.
Lum-Pa-Shuga. } MISS STEWART.

Dro-May-Jah. A high official .... MRS. NORTON.

Soldiers, Sailors, Indians, Members of the Tuscarora Light Guard, etc.

PROLEGOMENA

THE DEEPLY INTERESTING INCIDENT upon which this Drama is founded, occurred in Virginia, on Wednesday, Oct. 12, A.D. 1607, at twenty-six minutes
past 4 in the afternoon, according to the somewhat highly colored and
boastful narration of Capt. John Smith, the famous adventurer, backed by
the concurrent testimony of contemporaneous history; but subsequent re-
search has proved that either he was mistaken, or that *circumstance* had
unwarrantably plagiarized an affair which transpired at a much earlier date;
for, upon examining the contents of a wallet found in the vest pocket of the
man in armor, dug up near Cape Cod, an entire *epic poem* was discovered
upon the very same subject, which was written by a Danish Poet, the
Chevalier Viking, *Long Fellow* of the Norwegian Academy of Music, who
flourished Anno Gothami, 235.

The poem contains several square yards of verse, a fragment of which is
subjoined to show its peculiar *Finnish.*

THE SONG OF POCAHONTAS

> Ask you—How about these verses?
> Whence this song of Pocahontas,
> With its flavor of Tobacco,
> And the Stincweed—the Mundungus,
> With its pipe of Old Virginny,
> With the echo of the Breakdown,
> With its smack of Bourbon whiskey,
> With the twangle of the Banjo;
> Of the Banjo—the Goatskinnet,
> And the Fiddle—the Catgutto,
> With the noisy Marrowbonum.
> By one JONSMITH it was written,
> JONSMITH, the valiant soldier,
> Sailor, Buccaneer, Explorer,
> Hero, Trader, Colonizer,
> Gent, Adventurer, Commander,
> Lawyer, Orator, and Author,

Statesman, Pioneer, and Bagman.
Years he fought against the Moslem
Years he wore the captive's fetters,
Until, from a fond sultana
He received a Habeas Corpus.

Then, by way of relaxation,
He took passage on a steamer,
With a crew of Fillibusters,
Each with matchlocks and revolvers,
To take peaceable possession
Of some transatlantic region,
Sailed they on, they knew not whether,
Until, one October morning,
They incontinently blundered
On the shores of Tuscarora,
Near to Werowance, the palace
Of King POWHATAN, who flourished
In that section of the country,
Whereunto they were invited
By this hospitable monarch,
And remarkably well treated;
Until, fat with rice and pumpkins,
Buckwheatcake and sweetpotatoes,
Squashes, Homminy and Doughnuts,
They began to wax audacious,
And put on such airs and graces,
They were perfectly disgusting.

Now, the natives knowing nothing
Of the benefits intended
By this foreign congregation,
Who had come so far to show them
All how much they'd been mistaken;
In what darkness they were dwelling,
And how much obliged they were to
These disinterested people,
Who had journeyed to enlighten
Their unfortunate condition.
Through these potent triunited

Anglo-Saxon civilizers,
Rum, gunpowder, and religion.
Now, the natives, as I mentioned,
Didn't see the joke precisely
In the way it was expected,
They believing, simple creatures,
They could manage their own matters
Without any interference—
Thought the shortest way to settle
Those gratuitous advisers,
Would be quietly to knock them
On the head, like Bulls of Bashan.

It was then JONSMITH was taken
To be treated in such fashion,
Lying in a pleasant posture
On the ground, his head supported
By a chunk of Russ's pavement,
He looked round him with emotion.
King POWHATAN stood beside him,
With his battle-club tremendous,
Which around his head he flourished
To accelerate its motion,
So that when it swift descended
Upon JONSMITH's pericranium,
Then he wouldn't know what hurt him.
Thrice the fatal club was brandished,
And Jon. thought upon his mother,
Thought upon the prayer she taught him
When he first, a tiny urchin,
Bent his knee in simple wonder.
In that moment, all his childhood
Stood before him like a vision,
And he thought he was a "goner,"
When the King's remorseless purpose
Was immediately arrested
By a scream from Pocahontas.
Pocahontas, his own daughter—
She, the dove of Worocomoco,
The pride of Tuscarora,

Quickly laid her lovely tresses
On the pale cheek of the victim.
This mute eloquence of nature
To the heart of JONSMITH whispered,
You have yet a squeak, old fellow,
Now, &c. &c.

ACT I.

SCENE I: *Palace of Woramocomoco. Grand march of the Tuscarora Court. King enters with a great flourish.*

OPENING CHORUS

Air—*"King of the Cannibal Islands."*

KING AND CHORUS.

Oh! how absurd of people to prate,
About their mighty Kings so great,
They'd open their eyes to see the state
Of the King of the Tuscarora's.
As happy is he as King can be,
For from his Palace he can see,
The whole of his subjects merry and free,
So he takes his pipe contentedly,
Singing,
Smoking, joking Powhatan,
Tobacco it is the solace of man,
So let $\left\{\begin{array}{c}\text{subjects}\\\text{us}\end{array}\right\}$ puff as long as $\left\{\begin{array}{c}\text{you}\\\text{we}\end{array}\right\}$ can,
The King of the Tuscarora's.

KING. Well *roared* indeed, my jolly Tuscaroras.
Most loyal *Corps,* your King *encores* the *Chorus.*

[*Repeat Chorus*]

Bravo! We would with Shakspere say, *"that Strain again,"*
But it might strain your lungs, so we refrain.
It sooths my ear, like niggers from the South,
Stealing and giving odor; *they* sometimes do both,
Or like a pipe of the Nicotian leaf,
The true Nepenthe balm for every grief,
While other joys one sense alone can measure,
This to all senses gives extatic pleasure.
You *feel* the radiance of the glowing bowl,
Hear the soft murmurs of the kindling coal,
Smell the sweet fragrance of the honey-dew,

Taste its strong pungency the palate through,
See the blue cloudlets circling to the dome,
Imprisoned skies up-floating to their home.
I like a dhudieen myself.

    Col-O-Gog. I do not doubt it.

    King. I'll volunteer and sing a song about it.
To me 'twas by a wily Paddy whack sent,
Who had an axe to grind, hence the broad accent.

SONG—KING

Air—*"Widow Machree."*

Oh, wid a dhudieen I can blow away care,
    Oh, hone, wid a dhudieen!
Black thoughts and blue devils all melt into air,
Oh, hone! wid a dhudieen!
    If you're short any day,
    Or a note have to pay,
    And you don't know the way,
    To come out of it clean,
    From your head and your heart
    You can make it depart,
    Oh, hone! wid a dhudieen.

Oh, wid a dhudieen you recline at your ease,
    Oh, hone! wid a dhudieen!
Shut your eyes and imagine what pleasures you please,
    Oh, hone! wid a dhudieen!
    In dreams without sleep,
    All your senses to steep,
    While you're playing bo-peep
    Through each fairy-like scene,
    Undisturbed, I declare,
    By a single nightmare,
    Oh, hone! wid a dhudieen!

Oh, wid a dhudieen I'm as truly content,
    Oh, hone! wid a dhudieen!
What the rest of the world does I don't care a cent,
    Oh, hone! wid a dhudieen!
    Let some folks desire,

> To set rivers on fire,
> While some others admire,
> To run "wid de machine,"
> I've ambition enough,
> Just to sit here and puff,
> Oh, hone! wid a dhudieen!

Now that we have smoked ourself to proper dizziness,
Let us proceed at once to public business.
We must advance, though in the usual way,
Therefore, all laws that we made yesterday
We now repeal. We take the tax off Soap.

O-Po-Dil-Doc.   Soft Soap, so please your majesty, I hope?

King.   No, no, that saponaceous article escapes,
We've analyzed it with Professor Mapes,
And he told us, in terms quite scientific,
Soft Soap's considered a soft soporific.

Opo.   Sire, it's a lie!

All.   Order! Order!

King.   Can we believe our eyes?
We mean our ears.

Opo.   Are *not* soaps made from *lyes?*

King.   Oh! ah!

Col.   May it please your majesty, I rise
To a question of privilege. My honorable friend,
Being a *hard** himself, does not intend
An insult. May I ask in the word *lie,*
What vowel do you use, sir, *i* or *y?*

Opo.   Y sir, or *i* sir, search the vowels through,
And find the one most *consonant* to *you.*

All.   Order! Order!

Col.   To keep within the limits of debate.
Who stole the funeral cloth and coffin plate?

Opo.   Shut up, switch off, dry up, or go to bed!

Col.   I'll fling an inkstand at your honorable head!
If you had your desert, you'd *dine* in prison!

Opo.   And you'd have an asphyxiated weazen!

King.   Hollo! no more of this! at once have done!
Confound you, do you think that you're at Washington?

Opo.   My liege, in some authority I've read,

* "Softs" and "Hards" refer to political factions in 1855.

That it's within the rules to punch his head!

KING.   How is it, Mr. Speaker? We're in doubt.

SPEAKER.   Grotius,* cap 5, sec 3, says, fight it out.

                         [*Business, they prepare to fight*]

Out, out of this, some spot that none can trace,

Or *see* a *clew* to the *secluded* place.

COL.   Con*clude* it done! the deadliest weapon I can find,

I'll name!

OPO.   Nuff said, old top, I'll go it blind!

COL.   Blind you've been all your life, and deaf and dumb!

OPO.   Dum vivimus vivamus, what's your weapon?

COL.   *Rum*! [*A row outside.—Enter sergeant at arms*]

KING.   Sergeant at *arms,* say, what al*arms* the crowd?

Loud noise annoys us, why is it allo*wed?*

SER.   My liege, there is a band—

KING.   [*Starting up*] Of Minstrels?

SER.   No!

Of foreigners, just cast on Castle Garden.†

KING.   Oh!

For this relief, much thanks, it wouldn't pay.

That endless *bar*carole of old Dog Tray!

Who are those folks come here, without permission.

Something a *kin to Kin*ney's†† expedition!

This ranche they'd better vamouse mighty slick,

Old Nick's their destination, or *new Nic,*

Arauga, here they must not bore us,

As at *Sonora* with their bash *Sonorous,*

Conquering lands without a single resident,

Such a *Republic's* clearly without *precedent!*

SER.   Their leader is at hand, sire, at his back,

Four Knaves at least!

KING.**   They're found in every pack.

KING.   Produce this bold *adventurer,* whose *advent* here,

With our self-*interest* must *interfere.*

Meanwhile, we'll dip in Hoyle, and when you're back,

* Hugo Grotius (1583–1645) father of international law.

† A New York theatre first opened in 1845.

†† During the late winter of 1854 a Col. H. L. Kinney led a group of armed emigrants in an attempt to settle on the territory of Nicaragua; the Governor of Nicaragua protested against the invasion.

** There is a confusion of parts here; the line may have been spoken by OPO.

Know how to *deal* with such a dirty *pack*. [*Exit Sergeant*]
  SPEAKER.   How shall we receive them?
  KING.   As at the Opera House,
With a Chorus: there cannot be so proper a house
To set the fashion.

SONG AND CHORUS

Air—"Rosin the Bow."

KING.   Come forward here every rapscallion,
              And spread yourselves out in a row,
              While I ask that harmonious Italian
              La Manna* to rosin his bow.
CHORUS. La Manna, come rosin your bow, oh, oh,
              La Manna, pray rosin your bow,
              We aint got no forte-piano,
              Old beeswax, come rosin your bow.
KING.   Wake up, Mr. Trombone and Trumpet,
              And give us a jolly good blow,
              Like steam-engines out you must pump it,
              La Manna *will* rosin his bow.

[Chorus as before]

KING.   You chap with the blazing big fiddle,
              And you with the small one also,
               Keep your eye on the man in the middle,
              La Manna can rosin his bow.

[Chorus as before]

KING.   My friend of the side-drum and kettle,
              Be sure, and don't spare your el*bow*,
              But give us a thundering rattle,
              La Manna *will* rosin his bow.

[Chorus]
[Enter Captain John Smith and Retinue]

  KING.   What *manner* of *man are* you? A fillybustero!
Your *name* and *aim*, what brought you *there*, my *hero*?
  SMITH.   *Erratic* King, I might say *operatic*,
And, as I see, as *mellow* as *dramatic*,
My name is—
  KING.   Norval!†

* See title page of this play.
† Young Norval is the main character in *Douglas* (1756) by John Home (1722–1808).

SMITH. No, Sir! Smith—John Smith!
KING. Of Arkansas?
SMITH. No, Sire, that John's a myth.
KING. What *iron* fortune *led* you to our shores?
SMITH. *Ironic* Monarch, 'twas a pair of *oars*.
Between ourselves, though, if the truth be told,
Our *goal* we'll reach when we have reached your *gold*.
But, stop, and I'll enlighten your community,
I see [*Music in orchestra*] and hear a famous *opera-tunity*.

GRAND SCENA COMPLICATO

In the Anglo-Italiano Style

SMITH.   As you are o,
            The great cigar o,
            And high top loco,
            Among these folk o,
            It is but fair o,
            I should declare o,
            What brought me here o.
                'Tis easy told.
            You know my name o.
CHORUS.   Smith!
SMITH.   I hither came o,
            Impelled by fame o.
CHORUS. Bravo! Smith!
SMITH.   Or all the same o,
            The subtle flame o.
CHORUS. Go it, Smith.
SMITH.   The brilliant game o,
            Man's only aim o,
                To hunt up gold.
CHORUS. [*Abjure the Italian, and give themselves Ethiopian airs*]
            You're off the track, and you'd better go back,
                The golden dream is o'er;
            So order your hack and carry your pack
                From old Virginny's shore.
SMITH.   Oh, nar'ry a toe, will this child go,
                But open a grocery store,

And I'll never go back, 'till I've filled my sack
  On old Virginny's shore.

KING.   And what the *deuce* in*duce*d this scheme Utopian?
Proceed, we'll give *you rope* enough, *European!*
Though we don't relish being quite so *near*
As this, my *buck,* to such a *Buccaneer!*

SMITH.   Most potent, grave, and reverent old fellow,—
To use the words of that *black wight* Othello,
My very noble and approved good savage,
That we are come out here your lands to ravage,
It is most true: for this you see us banded.

                [*Indians rush at him—the King restrains them*]

KING.   I must confess, *sweet* sir, that you are *candid.*
You'll probably excuse us if we doubt it.
Pray how, sir, do you mean to set about it?

SMITH.   Easy enough: we have full powers to *treat.*

KING.   If that's the case, we'll take some *whiskey* neat.
You cannot *dash* our *spirits,* we are *proof*
Against such weakness!

SMITH.   Well, that's clear enough!
Ma*jestic* Savage, I was but in *jest*
Just now; you'll find, I *guess,* that I'm a *guest.*
It would be quite as *well* to *wel*come over
The seas we *clove* in hopes to live in *clover.*
Befriend us, and we'll try and be of use,
Even to cooking of your royal goose!

KING.   Don't put yourself into a stew, my friend,
My *Kitchen Cabinet** to that attend.
They know my constitution just like lawyers.

SMITH.   *Soyer* himself must yield to such top-*sawyers!*
But say, Great *Sachem,* don't re*fuse* this *fusion;*
To now *ill-use* us would be base *illusion!*
Puissant potentate, a*bridge* our *sighs,*
We *call on you* to let us *colonize.*
If this, most verdant Monarch, you will do,
A course of Sprouts we mean to put you through!

* A group of personal friends from whom Andrew Jackson sought advice during his first term as President rather than his regular Cabinet; they were dubbed the Kitchen Cabinet.

KING.   Sprout me no sprouts, irreverent *Suckers* all!
You can't lodge here, my friend, in *Short, at all!*
I can no *reason* in such *treason* see!
What! *share* my realm with you, mon *cher* ami?

SMITH.   Why not? We have the *brads* to buy your land,
Nails are a legal tender, they're on *hand,*
With beads and bracelets you shall all be crammed.

KING.   If I sell for brads, may I be d—ished!

SMITH.   In friendship with you we should like to tarry.
In proof of which I'm *ready* now to marry
Any *red* queen that in my way should fall,
I would a*ccept* her *Sceptre,* Crown, and all.
My hand is hers!

KING.   Your hand? You'd better p*ause!*
Among our *Indian maids* look out for Squ*aws!*
If any jokers dare to run their rigs
Near our *wigwams,* we're sure to *warm their wigs!*
What shall we do with them, the sons of topers?

SPEAKER.   Hang on the *outer* wall, the *inter*lopers!

ALL.   Hang them! Hang them!

SMITH.   What f*ault* have I committed? H*alt!*

KING.   Ha! Do you f*aulter?*

SMITH.   I fain would h*alt* before I reach the h*alt*er.
That *cord* is not my *line* in any sense,
I'd rather *not* be kept in such suspense!

KING.   You *shan't* be long! prepare yourself! But stay!
You'd rather not be hanged, I think you say?

SMITH.   I'm really fearful it would be a *drop*
Too much for me!

KING.   Perhaps you'd like a *chop*—[*With axe*]

SMITH.   Ill-manner'd *butcher,* you may *bet your* Crown
I'll fix your flint for you!

KING.   You simmer down!
Smith, you must die, as well as all *audacious*
Birds of passage that may migrate here!

SMITH.   *My gracious!*
Alas! then, did our *Nests* at home content us,
We would not now have been *Non est inventus!*
Mercy!

ALL.   No mercy!

KING. Not by any means!
My wrath they can't ap*pease,* so give them *beans!*

[*Indians rush at Smith*]

SMITH. Stay! *Soft!* Hold *hard!* One moment, if you please,
Until his Majesty a *secret sees!*

KING. A secret! What is it?

SMITH. Behold! [*Showing pistol*]

KING. [*Taking it*] We do! What's this?

SMITH. [*Taking it back*] A pistol, sire, I hope it will *suit* you
Should I *present* it!

KING. Ha! I see your *aim!*
By this you'd *buy* our silence, eh?

SMITH. The same!

KING. It's *curious!* What does it contain?

SMITH. Some potent pills.
And warranted to *cure* all mortal ills!
With a few doses we'll be undertakers
To rid you soon of all your *pains and acres!*

KING. I'd grieve with favors to be over*load*ed,
But with us kings such *cannons* are ex*plod*ed,
And so will take your physic. [*King fires pistol, drops it alarmed*]
Jarsey lightning! [*Rushes off, followed by Indians*]

SMITH. Hurrah! 'Tis clear, my friends, our skies are bright'ning!

BROWN. Let us be off—

SMITH. *Be off!* Recall that whine,
Or never *be off*icer of mine!
To leave our work half-done would be a pity,
And so we take possession of the city;
And as is usual in all such cases,
We'll nominate ourselves to all the places!
For Governor, John Smith!

BROWN. I second that!
It's carried; so be *seated!*

SMITH. [*Sitting*] Verbum *sat!*
I'd make a speech to you, but that's not needed,
For in to-morrow's *Herald* you can read it.
Be sure I'll make the best of this bad story,
To *gild* our *guilt* we've but to call it glory.
Success crowns every crime whoever bleeds,
Defies reproof and *sanctifies* misdeeds;

But pray excuse this personal reflection,
Unsuited to a primary election.
Propose your candidates.

   BROWN. Might I suggest,
A plan I've hit on that will be the best
To suit the present crisis. In this hat,
I've written all the names of all the fat
And juicy offices,—let each advance,
And in the *grab game* take an equal chance.

   ALL. Agreed! Agreed!

CONCERTED PIECE

Grab away
  While you may;
In this game, luck is all,
  And the prize
  Tempting lies
In the rich City Hall.

Grab away
  While you may;
For they say under Sam*
  Holds the "puss"
  And the "cuss"
Is as mild as a lamb.

Grab away
  While you may;
Every day there's a "job,"
  It's a fact
  By contract
All intact you may rob.

Grab away
  While you may;
For the pay never fear.
  Justice winks
  Aye, and blinks,
From the *dust* I scattered here.

                                        [Confusion at the Poll]

* In 1854 when the Know-Nothing Party was revived, members recognized each other with the question: "Have you seen Sam?"

BROWN. [*To Jones*] What are you? Treasurer?

JONES. No, vicey varcy.
I'm Secretary of State!

SMITH. I cry you Marcy!*
And you? [*To Junk*]

JUNK. An Alderman!

BUNTLINE. And so am I!

ANOTHER. And I!

SMITH. [*To Brace*] And what are you, old horse?

BRACE. I'm Mayor!

SMITH. No bed of roses is the Civic Chain!
See that your city fathers work their best,
When they're fatigued, why, let them have *arrest*.
Are you all satisfied?

BROWN. Um!—pretty well!

SMITH. Then let us try the tea—room for a spell—
Is there nothing we can do?
Meantime I'll chaunt the Marsellaise a la Rachel.†
We heard the Yankees this time, pretty dears,
They'll have to wait a couple of hundred years.

SONG

SMITH.   It is of a French actress I'm going to tell,
As came to America and her name it was Rachel
To play in deep Tragedies, both new ones and old
All for to make a fortune in silver and gold.

CHORUS. [*Anticipative of the way in which she intended to shovel in the specie*] Tol, de dol, &c.

SMITH.   Now she had a handsome Brother, and his name it was Félix,
Who thought he was posted in play-house politics,
For said he to himself—"I am just the right fel-
Low, to manage these Yankees uncommonly well.

CHORUS. [*Indicative of the proposed Modus Operandi*] Tol, de dol, &c.

SMITH.   "Oh," says he, "in the newspapers I'll come it strong,
All about the fine corps as I'm a fotchin' along,
They'll cost me some 5000 dollars a night,

---

* William L. Marcy (1786–1857), candidate for President in 1852, was made Secretary of State the following year.

† The French actress, Rachel, with her brother, Rapheal Félix, performed in America during the fall of 1855.

And to see so much go, will be a dolorous sight."

CHORUS.   [*Illustrative of the way he disbursed that large amount to the talented Company*] Tol, de dol, &c.

SMITH.   When the public I've told the tremendous expense,
They'll think that the prices are again to be immense,
Twenty-five dollars a ticket at least they must be,
They'll jump out of their skins when they find they're—
only *Three!*

CHORUS.   [*Delineative of the mad intoxication of the delighted populace*] Tol, de dol, &c.

SMITH.   Well, the doors they were opened, and the folks they walked in,
Think of *Félix's* feelinks, the domus was thin,
And it must be confessed that he looked rather *blue,*
When instead of *Three* dollars he had to take *Two.*

CHORUS.   [*Exemplifications of Félix's countenance as he reluctantly yielded to the pressure of the Press*] Tol, de dol, &c.

SMITH.   As the newspapers told him, the people flocked more,
And every one bought a French play-book at the door,
With their eyes on their books and their ears on the stage,
They thought they were *seeing* Rachel I'll engage.

CHORUS.   [*Descriptive of the studious way the general public avoided seeing the Great Actress*] Tol, de dol, &c.

SMITH.   Now all you nice folks as are fond of a play,
And like to be amused in a sensible way,
Don't you be deluded by fashion's sheep-bell,
But come *here* where our language you understand well.

CHORUS.   [*Suggestive of the grateful return made by the audience for this disinterested advice*] Tol, de dol, &c.

[*Smith is borne off in triumph*]

SCENE II: *Picturesque View in Jamestown, taken some time before it was built. Savage Play-Ground of a Tuscarora Finishing Institution. Vociferous irruption of Juvenile Squaw-lers. Enter Poo-Tee-Pet, Di-Mon-Di, Lum-Pa-Shuga, Dah-Ling-Duk, Nys-Kree-Tah,* O-You-Jewel, Hah-Jote-Lah,† Oso-Charming, &c. &c. &c.*

* Probably Luv-Lie-Kreeta as listed in Dramatis Personae.
† Omitted from Dramatis Personae.

CHORUS OF EMANCIPATED MAIDENS

Sing-sing away!
Sing-sing away!

Schools, but prisons are they say,
    Sing-sing away!
    Sing-sing away!
We'll have a *sing-sing* holiday. &c.

Poo-Tee-Pet.   I wish my Pa would send for me! Oh, dear!
    I'm *tired* of living so *retired* here,
    And I've school enough, I know that well,
    To set up any fashionable *belle!*
    Heigho! How can one stay here with content,
    The *present* time no *pastime* can *present!*
    No one to talk to of the Upper Ten.
    If it were even one of Brown's young men
    Just to begin with, for indeed the *fact* is
    I don't know how to flirt for want of practice.

Di-Mon-Di.   Isn't that dreadful, dear, I'm just the same,
    And for my part I think it's a great shame
    That we've no more young master's to impart
    The *rudest rudiments* of that fine art!
    Now, what's the use of drawing?

Poo-Tee-Pet.   I suppose
    That we may have some skill in *drawing beaux,*
    Let other people love to draw their spouses.
    That's horses' work—I'd rather much draw *houses.*
    Here comes Miss Pocahontas, haughty thing!
    Tossing her *crown* because her Pa's a *King!*
    Hum!—I know something!

Di-Mon-Di.   What?

Poo-Tee-Pet.   He must be *short,* or
    He'd have paid up, my dear, for her last quarter.
              [*Music. Enter, Po-ca-hon-tas, with Book*]

INTERNATIONAL SCENA—POCAHONTAS

[*Recitativo—Italiani doloroso*]

Pocahontas.   Sport am I of Fortune, no kind soul near to cheer me,
    I'm on the verge of dispair;
    Where can I turn me for comfort?
    Whence seek for sigh sympathetic?
        Ah! me unhappy!
        Most unhappy!

But my heart it will relieve, O,
   To sing from Hernani
   This recitativo!

INTER-ARIA NIGROQUAE

Where the idlers now are shopping
   In gay Fashion's round,
And at Banks, that are not stopping,
   You can hear the cold, gold sound.
All the world seems bright and cheery
   But sometimes 'tis mock
Oh! dark his lot who deals with Erie,
   For it's a fluctuating stock.*

CANTATA VARIOSO

Scenes that are brightest
   No one can trust,
When money's tightest
   Look to your dust.
Hope buoys, and carries us on,
   Carries us on through our days,
Carries us on like the pepper upon
   "Massachusetts Bays!"
     Oh! Heigh! Ho!
     Where is that beau
   Pa said he'd bring me a long time ago.

INTRUSIVE CHORUS. Oh! what a beau,
   What? A beau?
   Miss Pocahontas, you don't say so!

POCAHONTAS. Heigho! This *heated* term will shortly cease,
And these *school*-days to *warmer* ones give place!
I know not why it is, but since I've seen
Napoleon's life in *Harper's* magazine,†

* After the summer business depression of 1884, Erie Railroad stock fell drastically; by October the Company's debt was so large that the New York State Legislature provided some assistance.

† John S. C. Abott's "Napoleaon Bonaparte" appeared in *Harper's* from 1851 through 1854.

My soul enthusiastic, yearns to paint
The blissful deeds of some such *warlike saint!*
Since these heroic pages I've perused,
The stories that my childhood have amused
Are varnished with the fashions of last week;—
Never again with rapture shall I speak
Of dear Red Riding Hood, or Cinderella,
Or valiant little Jack the Giant *feller,*
Robinson Crusoe, or great Thumb the Small,—
This is the greatest *story* of them all!—
Oh! that it were my future fate to do
Some deed of desperation nice and new,
Something would startle all the world with fright,
That is, provided it *left* me all *right!*

    Poo-Tee-Pet. Girls, here come the teachers; hide your books,
Banish your smiles and put on your school looks!

    Pocahontas. I hate that School-Ma'am; she does look so sly.
She always has *a pupil in her eye!*

[*Enter Wee-Cha-Ven-Dar and Kros-As-Kan-Bee, Professors of haughty-culture, and trainers of the flowers of fashion*]

    Weech. Heads up, backs straight, chests out, and shoulders square!

    Kros. Miss Pocahontas, just look at your hair,
I never saw it in so vile a state!

    Poca. It *curls* so much that I can't keep it *straight.*

    Weech. Now, ladies, if you please, you'll get your bows.

    Poca. I wish I had one!

    Kros. Do turn out your toes!
You walk just like a *duck,* my dear, that's *flat!*

    Poca. Being a *duck,* you know, I can't help that!

    Kros. Come, ladies, please to recollect *time flies!*

    Poca. *Fly time's* too warm, I think, for exercise!

[*They try a Dance, and execute it with bows and arrows. Noise of pursuit without: Smith appears behind fence. Indian Girls cry, "A man!" and run off screaming, all but Pocahontas*]

    Smith. Believe me, there's no necessity at all,
Delicious *Schreechers,* for this sudden *Squall!*

Ah! Aid me, Maiden, pray!

   POCA.   Who are you?

Are you a *fugitive* come here to seek

A railway, underground?

   SMITH.   Not by a sight!

Alas! I'm only an unhappy *wight,*

Without a *shade* of *color* to excuse

Canadian Agents here to chalk my shoes;

Therefore my passage-money won't be figured,

For on that head Philanthropy is *niggard!*

   POCA.   Who is it this un*time*ly visit pays,

Breaking our school up before holidays?

   SMITH.   I'll tell you, thou un*fair*est of the *fair*

American Institution,—take a chair,

While my o'erloaded bosom I unfreight,

And all my *early* history re*late!*

[Gets chairs from entrance]

Most comfortable *chat*tels these to *chat* in,

Such chairs I ne'er thought to *sit* in here,—they're *sat*in!

'Tis now some twenty years—

   POCA.   I'll hear no more!

   SMITH.   You've cut my tale off!

   POCA.   Long ones are a bore!

Brief it must be, however you bewail it!

   SMITH.   I shall be *curt,* un*court*eous beauty, and *curt*ail it;

*Begin*ning with the *end* I had in view,

Which, upon my *soul,* was *sole*ly to see you,—

When from the *verge* of yon *Virgin*ny fence

I *saw* and *heard* a *sordid herd* advance!

From the *spot* I would have turned to flee

But one of the Chief's shadows *spotted* me,

And at his *back* the savage, at whose *beck*

They have a *knack* of tightening one's *neck!*

   POCA.   Can you tell who he was?

   SMITH.   The Chief? I can.

   POCA.   A King?

   SMITH.   The same.

   POCA.   His name?

   SMITH.   Is Powhatan*!* [*Pocahontas screams*]

Some near relation of yours, maybe?

Poca. Rather!
Nearer he can't be much, for he's my *Father!*
  Smith. The *deuce!*
  Poca. Have you been intro*duced?*
  Smith. Why,—No!
Not formally, but I have seen him though!
I visited his majesty's abode,
A portly savage, plump, and pigeon-toed,
Like *Metamora** both in *feet* and *feature,*
I never *met-a-more-a*-musing creature!
Now without fear my love I can avow it,
And *pop* the question boldly?
  Poca. My *pop* won't allow it,
I'll *bet* my life!
  Smith. My chance that *betters* still,
For being the *contrary* sex, you will!
In *fact, rare* princess, there's such *rarefaction*
Within my heart, such *"passional attraction,"*
That we must live together spite of fate,
For all impossibilities that congregate
Around us, my *free love* despises!
  Poca. Stop! One doubt within my heart arises!
A great historian before us stands,
Bancroft† himself, you know, forbids the *banns!*
  Smith. *Bancroft* be *ban*ished from your memory's shelf,
In spite of *fact* I'll marry you myself.
And happiness you'll have a better *show* for
With me, than should you wed that *low-bred loafer!*

DUET—SMITH AND POCAHONTAS

Smith.   My love is like a raging hot volcano,
        V*esuvius* in a fit of indigestion,
      And if you are so cruel as to *say no,*
        Insane, oh! I shall be without a question.
Pocahontas. Such volcanic affection 'twere just as well
        You'd keep, a little piano,
      That too *burning* a *mount* would a Cinderel-
        la make me, and I'm not a soprano.

* John Brougham, *Metamora* (1847); John Augustus Stone, *Metamora* (1829).
† George Bancroft (1800–1891), American historian.

But where's the use of jesting
    Or protesting,
With *you* this *un*ion never can take place.

SMITH.   'Tis vain my claim arresting
    Or contesting,
To gain you every record I'll efface.

BOTH.   Such an event must amusing be
    We have no fear in asserting,
For *chang*ing the current of History
    Would certainly be *divert*ing.

                                  [Noise of women without]

POCA. How from those prying *eyes* can I dis*guise* you,
My father's *prize* you'll be should he sur*prize* you!
[He puts on shawl and hat and pretends to read. Enter all the school. He mixes with them; they proceed towards gate as for a walk, in couples. Enter Powhatan and suite, Savagely. The girls are thrown into confusion]

WEECH. What is the meaning of this *rude* intru*d*ing?
KING. *Rude!* by the *rood* it means there's mischief broo*d*ing!
We *seek* a *suck*er who's *sec*reted here!
*Prod*uce him or *ind*uce him to appear,
Or by the towel, silver *fork* and spoon
You *fork*ed from me, I'll settle with you soon!
POCA. *[To girls]* Save him!
GIRLS. We will! *[They surround Smith]*
KING. You, daughter, come with me!
I'll settle you, too.
POCA. How, Pa?
KING. You shall see!
I've found a husband you must wed tonight!
POCA. Oh! my prophetic soul, *Bancroft* was right!
SMITH. *[Appearing]* What's that?
KING. Ha! we have you now, I guess!
POCA. Despair! Distraction!
SMITH. Here's a precious mess!
POCA. Where is my Smith, my love, my only one?
SMITH. My *Poca*hontas, ain't you *pok*ing fun?
KING. Here, dogs, we're in a snarl, so watch o'er us,
This blackguard guard and aid us in the chorus.

GRAND FINALE—AFFETTUOSA—FURIOSO—E. CONGLO MEROSO

CHORUS.   Come, let us now like watch-dogs bark,
              Come, let us now put out this spark,
              Come, let us raise a jolly row,
              And like the dogs of war, bow, wow.
SMITH.   I am plucked from fairy bowers,
              I am in misfortune's showers,
              Quite enough to wet a fellow through,
              Without an umbrella, too.
              Oh! I love this old man's daughter,
              Though inscrutable I've thought her,
              As the song of Hiawatha,
                  Writ by Long-fel-low.
POCA.   Oh! a little outsider, too,
              A little outsider view,
              A little outsider, your own child
              Appeals, dear dad, to you.
KING.   Mr. Smith, you're in a fix
              With your Don Giovanni tricks.
      But though you think yourself so much the dandy O,
              I'll bet you two to one
              You're almost as good as gone,
      For I'll use you up just like a stick of candy O.
OMNES.   It's all bosh and braggin'
                  All bosh and braggin'
                  All bosh and braggin'
              That you'll find, old "hoss."
                  Wait for the waggon,
                  Wait for the waggon,
                  Wait for the waggon,
              And you'll soon catch "goss."
                  END OF ACT ONE

ACT II.

SCENE I: *Isherwood's View of the Interior of a Wigwam. Powhatan pushes on Pocahontas with the parentally tyrannic air peculiar to irate potentates.*

DUETTO—IMPETUOSO

KING. Now, Ma'am, I have a notion,
    You can no longer rave,
This son of the *ocean oh shun,*
    A home on the salt sea, waive.

POCA. Your child, you may thus *seize, sir,*
    But sure as the *seas are* blue
I shall soon rescued be, sir,
    From you, and your *cruel crew.*

BOTH.   The prospect is inviting,
    Thus all my love requiting,
Of temper, you will find I have a share;
    Since you're bent on fighting,
    Thus all my prospects blighting,
I won't give in an atom, I declare.

KING. How sharper than a serpent's tooth, if one could find
Such things in serpents' heads, is an ungrateful child!
But here you shall remain till you've resigned
To settle *down* as I've made *up* my mind!
You'll make me *furious* if you yet re*fuse,*
Or venture to *eschew* the man I *choose!*

POCA. The king who would enslave his daughter so,
Deserves a hint from Mrs. Beecher Stowe!
Who is the *man,* sir; I de*mand* to know!

KING. Hey! day! Are we com*man*ded by our daughter!
I *taught* your *teach*ers to keep you much *taut*er
In hand! If thus the rein you mean to shy,
A *shy-reign* will be mine, methinks, bye-and-bye!
You must be *curbed a bit,* your doom's a prison,
If you don't quickly *hasten* to be *his'n!*

POCA. If thus you *wrong* my Woman's Rights, and mock

My griefs, your *offspring* will *spring off the dock!*
And mix my ardent spirits with cold water! [*Going*]
   KING.   Hold!
I did but jest, my *belle,* you shall be *told!*
The man's a Dutchman, deep as he can be,
In fact, as deep as the rolling Zuyder Zee.
A first-class venture, cautious and acute,
A widower, and good *shoe*maker to *boot!*
   POCA.   A widower! the proverb's here surpassed,
A *shoemaker* who looks beyond his *last!*
"*Ne sutor,*" sir, et cetera, so, you see
Such *suitor* is not likely to *suit* me! [*Rolff sings outside*]
   KING.   Here he comes; no *counterfeit* is he
Like Smith, whose very name's a *forgery!*
   POCA.   The other's worse by his own showing.
   KING.   How?
   POCA.   I heard him *uttering false notes,* just now!
   KING.   He's here! You see resistance now were idle;
His *bride* you shall be, so your temper *bridle!* [*Enter Rolff, smoking*]
   ROLFF.   Meine cootness gracious, was is das I see!
Is das meine loafley vrow as is to be?
   KING.   Yes, there's the prize, my son, go *in* and *win* her,
While, to escape the *din,* guess I'll go in to *din*ner.

GRAND SCENA PERTURBATO

Aria—"*Hibernoso affettuosamente.*"

   POCA.   Aurora, no more will I hail thy first dawn,
             No more hear the soul-stirring cry of "hot corn,"
             I have nothing to do now, but languish and die,
             "Crushed out" as I am by my Pa's cruel*ty.*
             But I'm not so *domestic* a thing, on my life,
             As ever to be yon *brown Hollander's* wife.
             No, rather than that, a deep hole I would bore
             In my heart, and behold bright Aurora no more,
             And oh! if I'm forced like poor DINAH, to die,
             By going, and taking a cup of cold *py*—
             —*zon,* no VILLIKINS will I leave here to deplore,
             That this child should behold bright Aurora no more.

Cantata—*"Giojoso et amoroso."*

ROLFF.   Oh peutivool girl,
Mein prave Indian bearl,
Love runs like a squirrel
     Meine heart up and down.
Oh don't look so freezy,
Uneezy and breezy,
Meine vrow you must be see
     In spite of your vrown.
Oh peutivool creeter,
I'd fling at your feet your
Audacious beseecher,
     Now bobbin around.
But you mustn't be freezy,
Uneezy or breezy,
Meine vrow you must be see
     In spite of your vrown.

Song—*"doloroso et petulento."*

KING.   'Tis a hard blow to suffer
     When sad and alone,
Some poor aged buffer
     Sits by his hearthstone,
No flour in his kitchen,
     No fire-water nigh,
His complexion to nourish
     By a drop in his eye.

TOGETHER.   In our cane brakes of an afternoon,
We sometimes go for to hunt the coon,
And from experience I declare
He ain't an easy bird to snare.
     Clar's his action,
        Old coon, sly coon
        Old Virginia never tire.

POCA.   Appeal is useless! What words could I utter,
To mollify this firkin of Dutch butter!
Oh! tell me, was that sentence that my Pa
Made use of, true, that I'm to wed you?

ROLFF.   Yah!

Poca. But if I say I love another?

Rolff. Psha!

Poca. You wouldn't force me to espouse you?

Rolff. Yah!

Poca. Was ever maiden's love so sublimated!

Single, ere this, and now thus *doubly*-mated!

But, once for all, sir, know I'm not inclined

To wed a *beau* with such a *narrow* mind!

Dutchman, depart! The honor I resign;

Leave me, or else, *believe* me, you shall rue it!

Rolff. Nein!

SONG—ROLFF

[*With Tyrolean fixins*]

Like the Tyrolese singers, so gallant and gay,

I'll sing you a song in the Tyrolese way,

Fol de dol, de dol lay—it's a very fine day;

It doesn't much matter—you know, what I say.

[*Here follows an exhibition of tracheotomous gymnastics, which must be hard to be properly appreciated*]

I wish from mein soul all de rocks round about

Would to *sausages* turn, and the trees to *sourcrout.*

The ocean's vast bowl into *lager bier* roll

And I was an earthquake to swallow the whole.

[*More vocal gymnastics*]

And then for mein pipe I'd *Vesuvius* fill full

Of *kanaster* and through a *pine tree* take a pull

And after that, p'raps, for fear of mishaps,

I'd toss down *Niagara Falls* for mein *schnapps.*

[*Gymnastics again*]

Rolff. It ain't no use to crumble, zo you zee

Mein peauty, you must gome along mit me!

[*She struggles wildly with the destroyer of her peace, to corresponding Music, marked, and melo-dramatic*]

Poca. Un*hand* me, thou un*hand*some caitiff!

Rolff. Nein!

It's no good kicking, now, you must be mine!

Poca.   Where shall I turn?

[*Breaks from him distractedly—suddenly beholds the members of the Or-chestra and appeals to them*]

              Can you look calmly on
And see thus shameful *Overture* begun,
Yet take no part! I cannot call you *men,* or
You'd out-shout the *treble base*ness of the *tenor!*
Thou rude a*ssailer,* must I storm without *avail?*

                              [*Smith jumps in at the window*]

    Smith.   Avast! Not when a *sailor's* within *hail!*

[*Tableau of triumphant innocence, and disconcerted Dutch villany. Smith continues ora-tar-ically*]

Sheer off at once, you ugly-looking craft,
Or, damme, if I don't rake you fore and aft!
Perhaps I'd better kill him, love?—Here, stay!
What do you think?

    Poca.   It might be the best way.

    Smith.   Of course it will be. So, audacious rival,
Prepare, at once, to die!

    Rolff.   To *die!* Der *Deifil!*
Help, murder, help!

[*Smith, proceeding to annihilate him, is intercepted by* Powhatan]

    King.   Holloa! What's the row?

    Rolff.   Dat dere tam Smit has dook away mien vrow!
And vos vant do gill me do pezite!

    King.   Dear me, is that all? I'll soon set it right.
Children, come here; I've changed my mind.

                              [*Shaking hands with Smith*]

    Rolff.   What's dat?
You shakes him by de hand? [*King winks at Rolff*]
Oho! I smells a rat. [*Aside*]

    King.   I'll fix him. [*Aside*] Smith, we to our daughter's choice
Lend the loud sanction of our Royal voice.

    Smith.   Your *voice* allo*wed,* but has your heart re*lent*ed?

    King.   If in our simply *tent* you'll live con*tent*ed.

    Smith.   To an *extent intense.* King, you're a brick!

    Rolff.   Mein vrow! mein Got! dis is a purdy drick.

    King.   *Demmy John. cork up!* Now, daughter dear, prepare,

With orange wreaths *array* your *raven* hair;
To *prove* I love *you,* Smith, before you wed,
We'll take a *proof* impression of your head,
In our approved new lithographic style.
   SMITH. With all my heart; but if you harbor guile,
My *tars* will make a *target* of your head.
   KING. Upon the honor of a king!
   SMITH. 'Nuff said.

     QUARTETTE—KING, SMITH, ROLFF, and POCAHONTAS

   Fill now a flowing glass
      We would, without doubt, sir,
  But as we've none, alas!
     We must do without, sir.
       We'll live, never fear,
       In harmony here.
KING. (Poor John Smith is very grateful.)
CHORUS. As lazy as monks in a cloister.
KING. (Grief he's not now troubled with.)
CHORUS. Both soft shells and hard
      We here disregard.
KING. (He's gentle and resigned,
    And resolved to go it blind.)
CHORUS. So we get our fair share of the oyster.
KING. Oh, what a fool is poor John Smith!

                           [Poco a poco discretioni]

SCENE II: *School Ground as before. Poo-Tee-Pet looking cautiously.*

   POO-TEE-PET. Come, girls, we'll have our little confab here,
No prying principals can interfere.
I've dreadful news for you!
   DI-MON-DI. You don't say so!
What is it, dear; I'll die if I don't know.
   GIRLS. And so will I. And I.
   DI-MON-DI. For my part, I can't guess
What it can be that gives you such distress.

Do let us know at once.

    GIRLS. Do—do!

    POO-TEE-PET. I will.

Imagine the extreme of human ill.

    LUMP-A-SHUGA. Are the new bonnets worn on the head?

    DI-MON-DI. There's been a fight, and all the *men* are dead.

    POO-TEE-PET. Not quite so bad as either, but behold!

A tale of horror in this note is told!

    DI-MON-DI. Do tell!

    LUMP-A-SHUGA. I want to know!

    DI-MON-DI. What can it be?

    POO-TEE-PET. Miss Pocahontas tells me here, that she is going to marry.
[*All laugh*]

    DI-MON-DI. What a heavy blow!

    POO-TEE-PET. But not the man she's in love with!

    GIRLS. Oh!

    POO-TEE-PET. At Union Square, this afternoon, 'tis fated,

The wrongful *rites* are to be consummated!

The awful moment is almost at hand,

But as this *scand*alous affair I've *scann*ed,

If you'll but *second* me in what I say,

Our hands will show them what's the *time o' day!*

You can *wind up* this business as you like,

If at the proper instant you but *strike!*

Strike! like the steel of Halleck's brave Bozzaris,*

Strike! as the newest fashions do in Paris,

Strike! for your rights, your homes, and kitchen fires;

Strike! like a crowd of feminine Tom Hyer's.†

    GIRLS. We will! Hurrah! Down with mankind in general!

    DI-MON-DI. A very striking denouement, indeed,

If we could only *see* how to proc*eed*.

    POO-TEE-PET. I have got leave, to-day, for our diversion,

To go *on* a toxopholite excursion.

A female target party—'twill be fine

Before they can suspect our deep design,

By stratagem to get them to desist, or

Else by force of arms *assist* our *sister*.

The plan is dangerous, and now you know it,

---

  *Reference to a poem by Fitz-Green Halleck (1790–1867) entitled "Marco Boz-
zaris" (1825).

  † Tom Hyer was a noted pugilist.

Are you all game to see it through?

GIRLS. We'll *go it!*

POO-TEE-PET. Now, let's be off, as we've no time to *lose.*

DI-MON-DI. Those gentlemen can keep time, I suppose. [*To Orchestra*]

POO-TEE-PET. Then, if you please, as we've good time before us.

We'll just take time enough to sing a chorus. [*Addressing Leader*]

CHORUS

Air—*"Pop goes the Weazle."*

As we're going on a train
    We must see and load a
Hamper with a drink of *Maine*
    Pop goes the soda.

Hampered thus, no Indian corn
    Can we now forebode, a
Bumper fill then, (in a horn),
    Pop goes the soda. [*Exeunt omnes*]

SCENE LAST: *Union Square in the City of Worowocomoco. The assembled Upper Tendom of Tuscarora, discovered.*

CHORUS

Air—*"Hark 'tis the Indian Drum."*

Hark 'tis the in*gine* bell,
    Look out for the locomotive.
We off the track must go.
        Though
His majesty is rather slow,
    He must be how come you so,
With Smith's New England rum:
    The rum, the rum, &c., &c.

[*Enter Pocahontas, evidently in very indifferent spirits, her overburthened soul bursts forth in melody*]

Air—*"Notturne, Grazioso vel Filosofoso"*

POCA. Oh, some are right
    Who don't invite

Within their vest
So dangerous a guest,
   As *love* that hies
     To this abode,
   And heavy lies—
     Dyspeptic load.
   It sets one frying
   And sadly sighing,
You can't lodge here, no way,
   So *love,* good day,
   'Twill never pay
   To let you stay,
So *love,* good day, good day, good day,
   I'm better off without thee,
         Verily.
   And do not care about thee,
         No, not I. [*She goes off sadly*]
[*Enter Powhatan and Smith, Rolff creeping cautiously after*]
   KING. Here's where my artists dwell, a race gregarious,
Cheering their up *hill* life with mirth *hil*arious.
Smith, where are all your sailors? Safe, I trust?
   SMITH. Yes! *Safe,* by this time, to be on a *bust!*
   KING. Do none of your brave *hands* about here linger?
   SMITH. I need no *hands* while I those *arms* can *finger.*

[*Rolff, who has stolen behind Smith, suddenly snatches his pistols, one of which he hands to Powhatan, producing a perilous and plagisarous situation, A la Rob Roy—Smith served with a "ne exeat" at every opening, by the servitors of the King, and finally bound over to a strong chord in the Orchestra*]

   ROLFF. Friend Smith, you're *double-sold!* You lose your wife!
   KING. Likewise, to a *dead* certainty, your *life!*
   SMITH. Such hospitality was ne'er surpassed.
Invited to a *feast* and thus *made fast!*
But, as to you, base cobbler, soon to pay
For what's *occurred,* I'll find a ready *way!*
There's not a *red* marauder in the land
But henceforth *seeks* your *hide* to have it tanned!

Think on't, and tremble to your marrow's pith!
Judas! You haven't yet sub*dued* JOHN SMITH!
  KING. Don't make a *Judy* of yourself!
  ROLFF. Meine friend!
Your *thread* of life is *waxing* to an *end!*

[*A Scotch Indian march, with variations and situations, singularly similar to those which have occurred in similar situations*]

  KING. Now, that our finishing touches may be shown,
Bring forth our finest lithographic stone!

[*He is obeyed with servile alacrity.—Flourishes a huge club*]

I said I'd take your head off!
  SMITH. But I swear,
You didn't hint about that sketch *club* there!
  KING. Disappointed in the likeness you can't be!
  SMITH. 'Twould be more *strik*ing if my hands were free!
But as I'm bound to let you have your way,
A few last words, I trust, you'll let me say?
  KING. We're *tied* to *time,* and *time* and *tide* won't wait,
You must *die early* so you can't *dilate!*
Our *Indian* laws are *some,* there's no receding!
  SMITH. Why, what an Indian *summary* proceeding!
  KING. A sentence, come, prepare!
  SMITH. Hold on a spell
Fell tyrant!
  KING. Ha! What's that?
  SMITH. I mean, *old "fel,"*
You wouldn't cut a *fellow's thread?*
  KING. That's *so!*
I do assure you, you shan't feel the blow!
Old *Tar,* to-night in *Tar*tarus you'll sup!
  SMITH. Life's a *conundrum!*
  KING. Then lie *down, and give it up!*
  SMITH. It's a hard *pill*—but a much harder *pi*llow! [*Reclining*]
[*Pocahontas rushes in heroineically distressed and dishevelled, followed by sailors*]
  POCA. Husband! For thee I *scream!*
  SMITH. *Lemon* or *Vanilla?*

Poca. Oh! *Fly* with me, and quit those vile dominions!
Smith. How *can* I fly, beloved, with these pinions?

Duet—Smith and Pocahontas—*"Prima Donna Waltz"*

Smith. Although a *bird* am I,
        And sometimes do get high—
            A pair of wings
            Are essential things
        Before a bird can fly.
Poca.   Oh! dearest, die I must,
        My heart, just like pie crust
            Is breaking in pie—
            Ces, only to see
        How *fowl*ly my *bird* is trussed.
Smith. A *verse* to *add,* I'm not *adverse* to
        Though *adversity's* a curse—so
        Come what may—fate can't do worse, oh
            Farewell.
Poca. Loose him, and let him be my spouse!
King.   Not I,
        Such an *alliance* would be all *a lie!*
        On no ac*count,* can I run *count*er to
        Virginia records which relate to you.
        I'm very sorry, Smith, but you must die! [*Music*]
Smith. Wait 'till the Target Party passes by!

[*Enter Poo-Tee-Pet and all the Indian women. They execute sundry manoeuvres and finally form a hollow square around Smith, very pointedly pointing their arrows at the King and company*]

  King. Hollo! Stop that! My goodness! I do declare!
Those arrows make me *quiver!*—as you were!
What *are* you, that thus outrage all propriety?
  Poo-Tee-Pet. The Anti-marry-folks-against-their-will Society!
  King. Why come you here?—as sorrowful spectators?
  Poo-Tee-Pet. No! on the contrary, we're *very glad*iators!
        For Freedom every heart with ardor glows,
        On Woman's Rights we're *bent,* and *bent* our bows!
        Your daughter dear must marry whom she may,
        Daughters, you know, should *always* have their *way!*

KING. What's to be done? I'm puzzled in good sooth,
I love my daughter, but can't warp the truth!
SMITH. You've *ample* means, ex*amples* you don't lack,
Didn't Shakspeare give King Richard a crook back,
For fear bold Queen Elizabeth would frown,
Whose grandpapa had cracked his Royal crown!
In our day, isn't every *corn*er rife
With Hot Corn heroines ne'er seen in life?
Don't Mr. Abbott make that bloody Tartar,
Napoleon Buonaparte, a Christian martyr?
If these don't satisfy you?
KING. No, they don't!
SMITH. I'll fight him for the maiden!
ROLFF. No, you won't!
SMITH. Draw lots, shake props, shoot pistols, or petards,
Or *stake* her *hand* upon a *hand* of cards!
KING. Ha! ha! there's sense in that; you're on a track
That *suits* us to a *T*. Who's got a pack? [*They all produce the documents*]
Stay! here's a table—sit upon the edge. [*They sit upon a stone*]
He's done! [*Aside*] What shall the game be, Smith?
SMITH. Old Sledge!* [*All crowd round anxiously watching the game*]

CHARACTERISTIC CONCERTED PIECE

CHORUS. Now for a jolly encounter at High, Low, Jack, and the
Game.
KING AND SMITH. The Queen!
A trump!
A better!
The Ten!
That's good for my Jack!
CHORUS. Oh! what a jolly encounter at High, Low, Jack, and the
Game.
KING AND SMITH. A trump!
Another!
That's low!
That's so.
And that's the best card in the pack!

* A variety of "all fours" game, known under several names in America.

Poca. Oh! Mr. Hoyle,
    All his toil
    Prithee spoil.
Chorus. Give him fits.
Poca. Oh! Master, pray
    Mind the way
    That you play.
Chorus. Give him fits.
Smith. I've won the game,
      Upon my life;
    And better still,
      I've won a wife!
    At High, Low, Jack,
      You cannot shine—
    So take the pack,
      The maid is mine.
    I'm bound to play all night,
      I'm bound to play all day;
      I'll bet my money on the High, Low, Jack,
      For ever, if thy hand's my pay.
King. Mr. Smith, I must acknowledge, I'm a sure gone coon,
    I'm dished, and feel exactly like a used-up spoon:
    Though I thought the game to play to another sort of tune,
    And beat you, too, before you'd say Jack Robinson.
Omnes Coda. He's won the game, &c.
Smith. Hurra! I've won the game!
King. Well, that's a fact!
Rolff. Der's sheating round dis board! de gards was backed!
Boo hoo! I'm zwindled! [*Cries*]
King. Just you stop that blubber,
Bub, or cut in for an *Indian rubber!* [*Flourishing club*]
Smith. I have *won fairly,* I appeal to you. [*To King*]
And *fair one,* I have *fairly won you, too,*
So let us *two* make one.
Poca. Papa, you've heard?
King. It likes me not, but I must keep my word;
There, take her!—that, I think's the usual thing—
               [*Joining their hands patriarchally*]
Now, let your voices *round* the *circle ring.*
Our son-in-law, three cheers, and make them tell!

Hip, hip, hurrah! [*They shout*] Tiger! [*They roar*]
Indian yell! [*They scream*]

SMITH.   Old King of Clubs, you are a jolly trump!
And don't you be so downcast, you Dutch pump;
All future history will see you righted.
With her, in name alone, I'll be united.

POCA.   How long the union may exist, depends
On the impartial verdict of our friends.

KING.   Give your consent, and all dispute will cease,
A citizen's first duty is to *keep the peace.*

SMITH.   So, pray *keep this one,* not in *bonds* too tight,
But suffer it to run through many a night.

Grand Finale—"*A la Grec.*"

KING.   And now we've done our duty here,
    We hope and trust that you'll not fume, or
    Fail to give a parting cheer,
    But take our bad jokes in good humor—
        Tow row row,
        People will you now
      Take our bad jokes in good humor,
        Now, now, now. [*Da Capo Chorus*]

SMITH.   Good people all, both great and small,
    Now, you and your kind friends we *want,* as
    Often as you please to call
    On Captain Smith and Pocahontas.
        Tow row row,
        Lenity allow,
      Captain Smith and Pocahontas,
        Now, now, now.

TABLEAU AND CURTAIN

America's Lost Plays

VOLUME IX

CHARLES HOYT

Plays: *A Bunch of Keys, A Midnight Bell, A Milk White Flag, A Trip to Chinatown, A Temperance Town*

EDITED BY DOUGLAS L. HUNT

VOLUME X

BRONSON HOWARD

Plays: *Knave and Queen (Ivers Dean), Old Love Letters, Hurricanes, Baron Rudolph, The Banker's Daughter, One of Our Girls*

EDITED BY ALLAN G. HALLINE

VOLUME XI

STEELE MacKAYE

Plays: *Rose Michel, Won at Last, In Spite of All, An Arrant Knave*

EDITED BY PERCY MACKAYE

VOLUME XII

ROBERT MONTGOMERY BIRD

Plays: *The Cowled Lover, Caridorf, News of the Night, 'Twas All for the Best*

EDITED BY EDWARD H. O'NEILL

VOLUME XIII

RICHARD PENN SMITH

Plays: *The Sentinels, The Bombardment of Algiers, William Penn (frag-ment), Shakspeare in Love, A Wife at a Venture, The Last Man*

EDITED BY H. W. SCHOENBERGER AND RALPH H. WARE

VOLUME XIV

MISCELLANEOUS

Plays: *Metamora*, by J. A. Stone, *Tancred*, by J. A. Stone (one act), *Signor Marc*, by J. H. Wilkins, *The Battle of Stillwater*, by H. J. Conway, *The Crock of Gold*, by Silas S. Steele, *Job and His Children*, by Joseph M. Field, *The Duke's Motto*, by John Brougham, *The Spy*, by Charles P. Clinch, *The Usurper*, by J. S. Jones

EDITED BY EUGENE R. PAGE

VOLUME XV

ROYALL TYLER

Plays: *The Island of Barrataria, The Origin of the Feast of Purim, Joseph and His Brethren, The Judgment of Solomon*

EDITED BY ARTHUR WALLACE PEACH AND GEORGE FLOYD NEWBROUGH

VOLUME XVI

HISTORICAL AND ROMANTIC PLAYS

Plays: *Monte Cristo (as played by James O'Neill), Hippolytus*, by Julia Ward Howe, *Mistress Nell*, by George Hazelton, *Becky Sharp*, by Langdon Mitchell, *The Warrens of Virginia*, by William C. deMille

EDITED BY J. B. RUSSAK

VOLUME XVII

HENRY C. DeMILLE

IN COLLABORATION WITH DAVID BELASCO
AND CHARLES BARNARD
Plays: *The Main Line, The Wife, Lord Chumley, The Charity Ball, Men and Women*

EDITED BY ROBERT HAMILTON BALL

VOLUME XVIII

DAVID BELASCO

Plays: *La Belle Russe, The Stranglers of Paris, The Heart of Maryland, The Girl I Left Behind Me, Naughty Anthony*

EDITED BY GLENN HUGHES AND
GEORGE SAVAGE

VOLUME XIX

BARTLEY CAMPBELL

Plays: *The White Slave, My Partner, The Galley Slave, Fairfax, The Virginian*

EDITED BY NAPIER WILT

VOLUME XX

AUGUSTIN DALY

Plays: *Man and Wife, Divorce, The Big Bonanza, Pique, Needles and Pins*

EDITED BY CATHERINE STURTEVANT